Heathen Art
Portfolio by Benjamin Long
January 2013

Welcome to a new year, last years portfolio was rather reflective of the Art that I had done for that year. This year is a time for change like any other year and there will be attempts at innovative new drawing techniques in the development of my style. Fear not the old style is not going to disappear, yet last year I focused on gradient shading, and this year I am going to attempt to vary hatching styles in my drawings to produce innovative new effects that would be rather aesthetically pleasing to the person appreciating the art. I thank you and here is forty pages of art by Illustrator Benjamin Long...

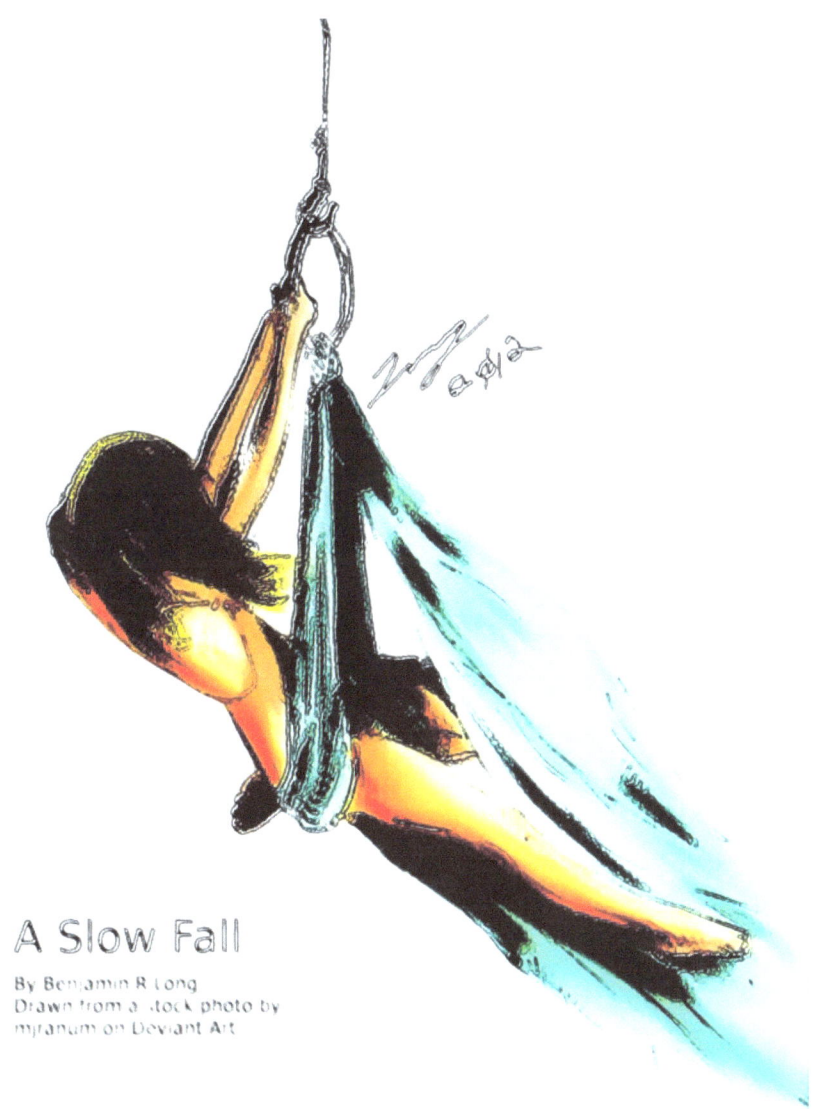

A Slow Fall

By Benjamin R Long
Drawn from a stock photo by
mjranum on Deviant Art

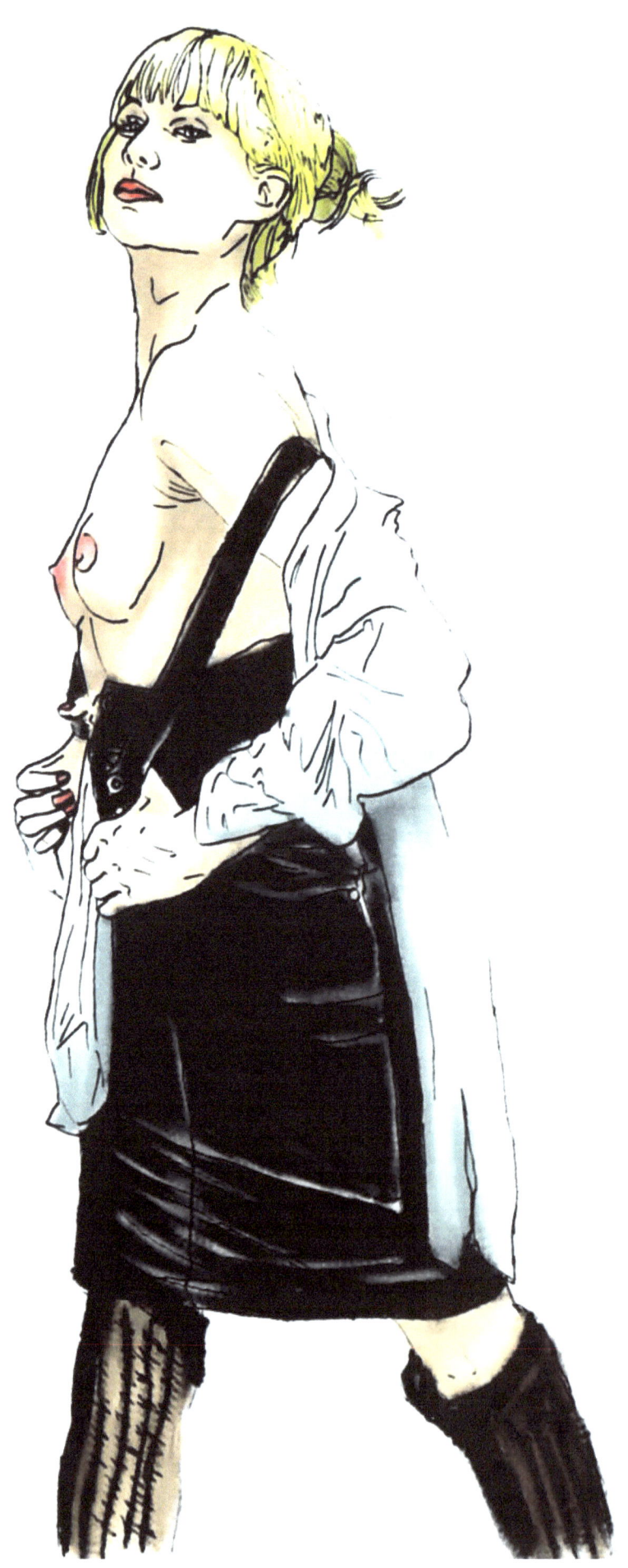

Beach Pinup

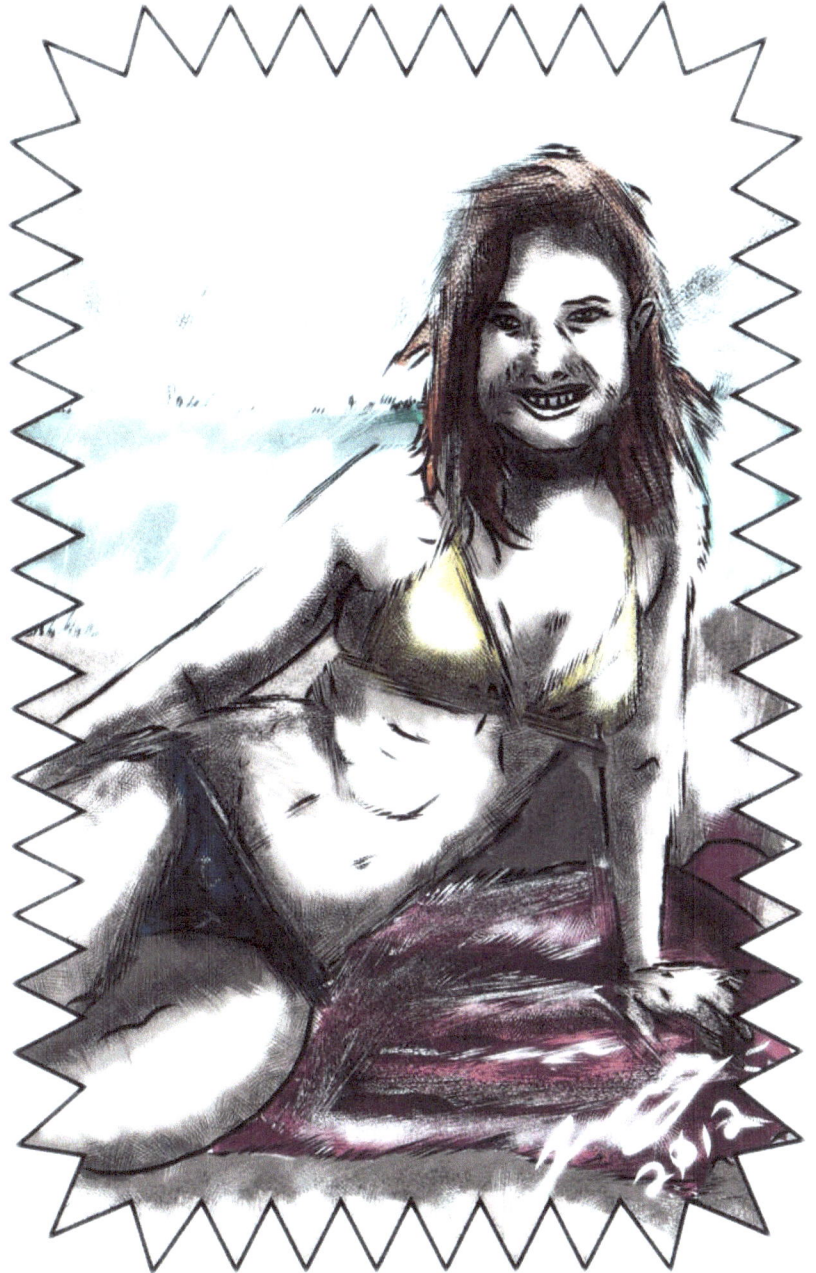

Illustrated by Benjamin Long 2012

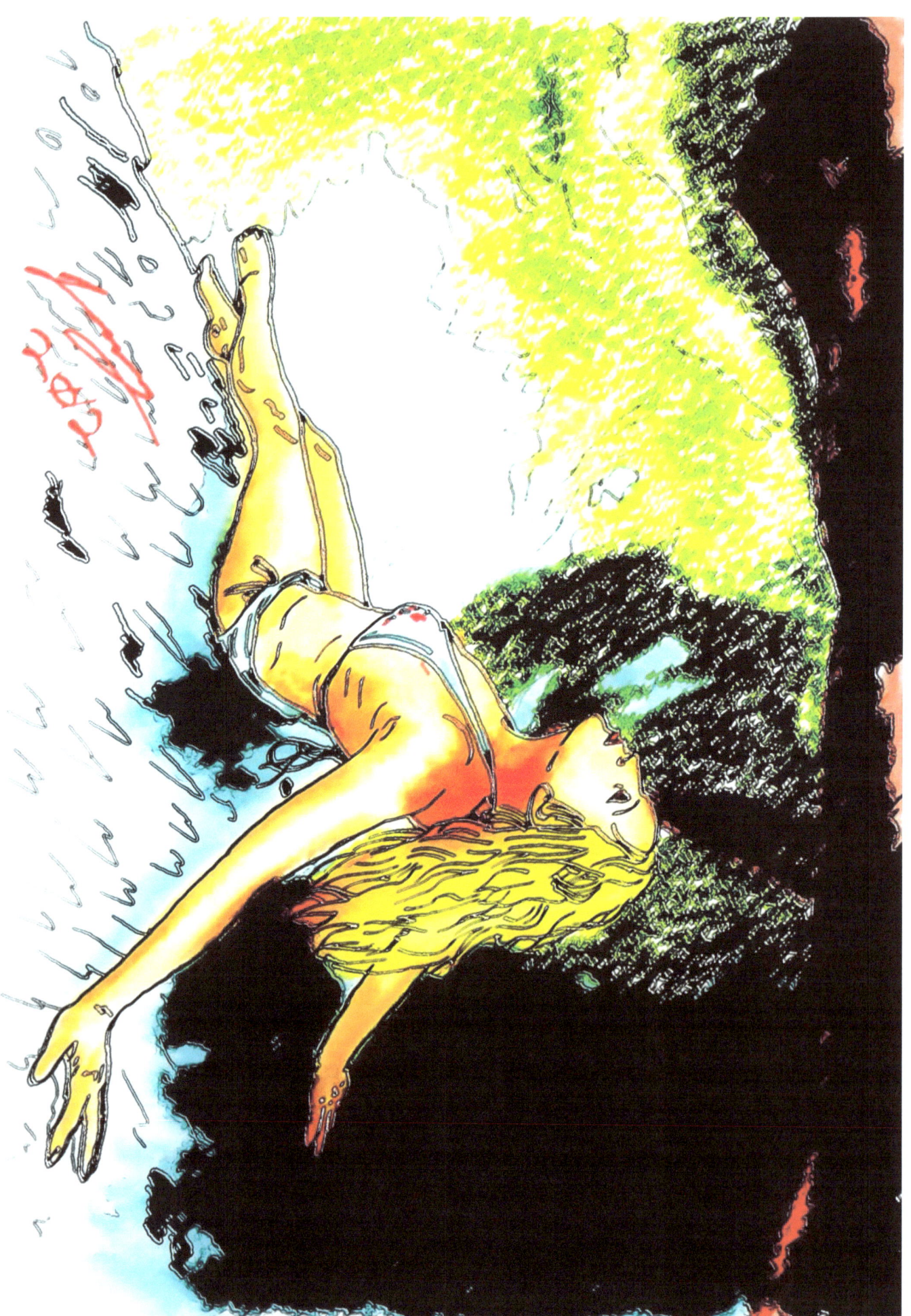

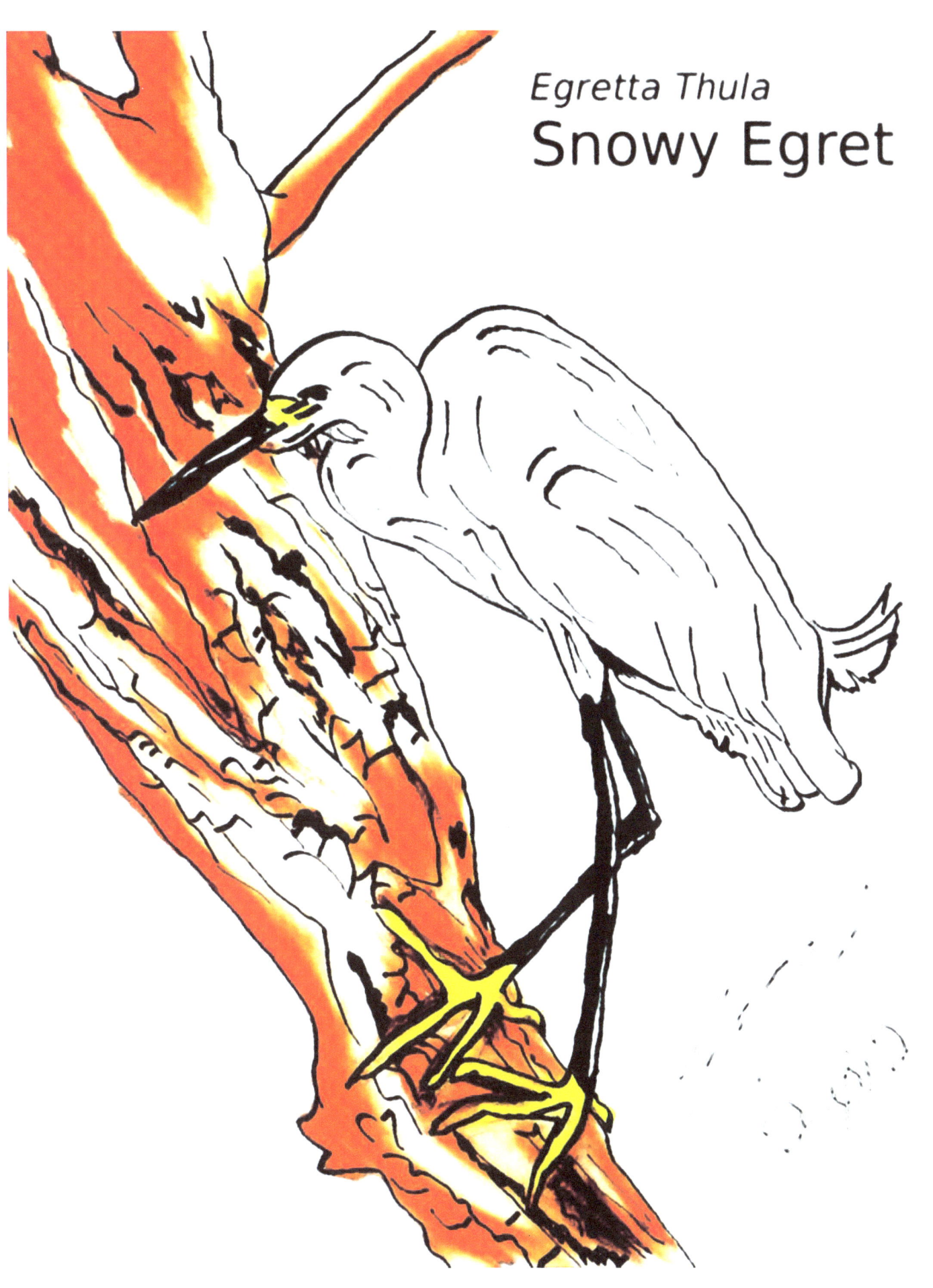

Egretta Thula
Snowy Egret

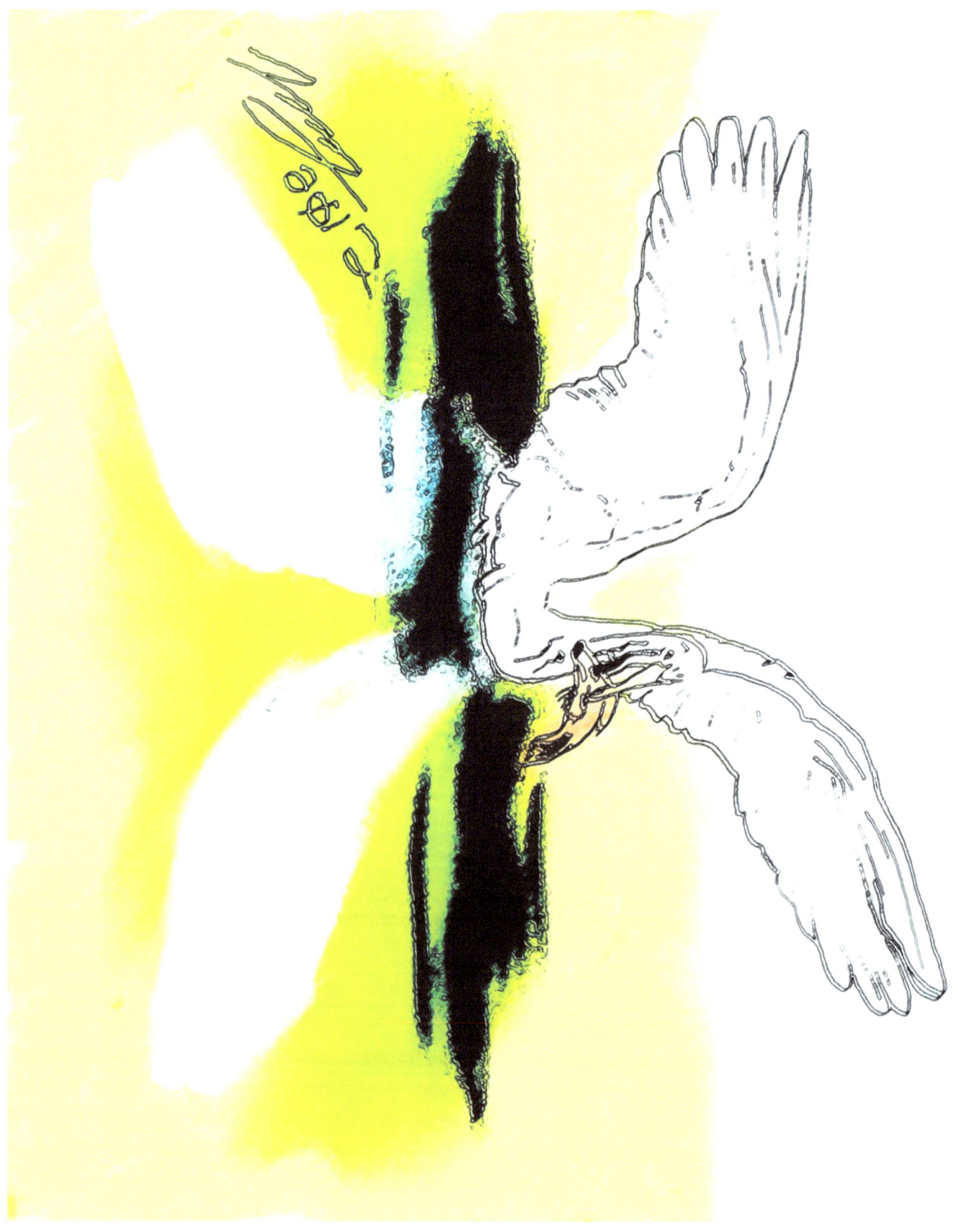

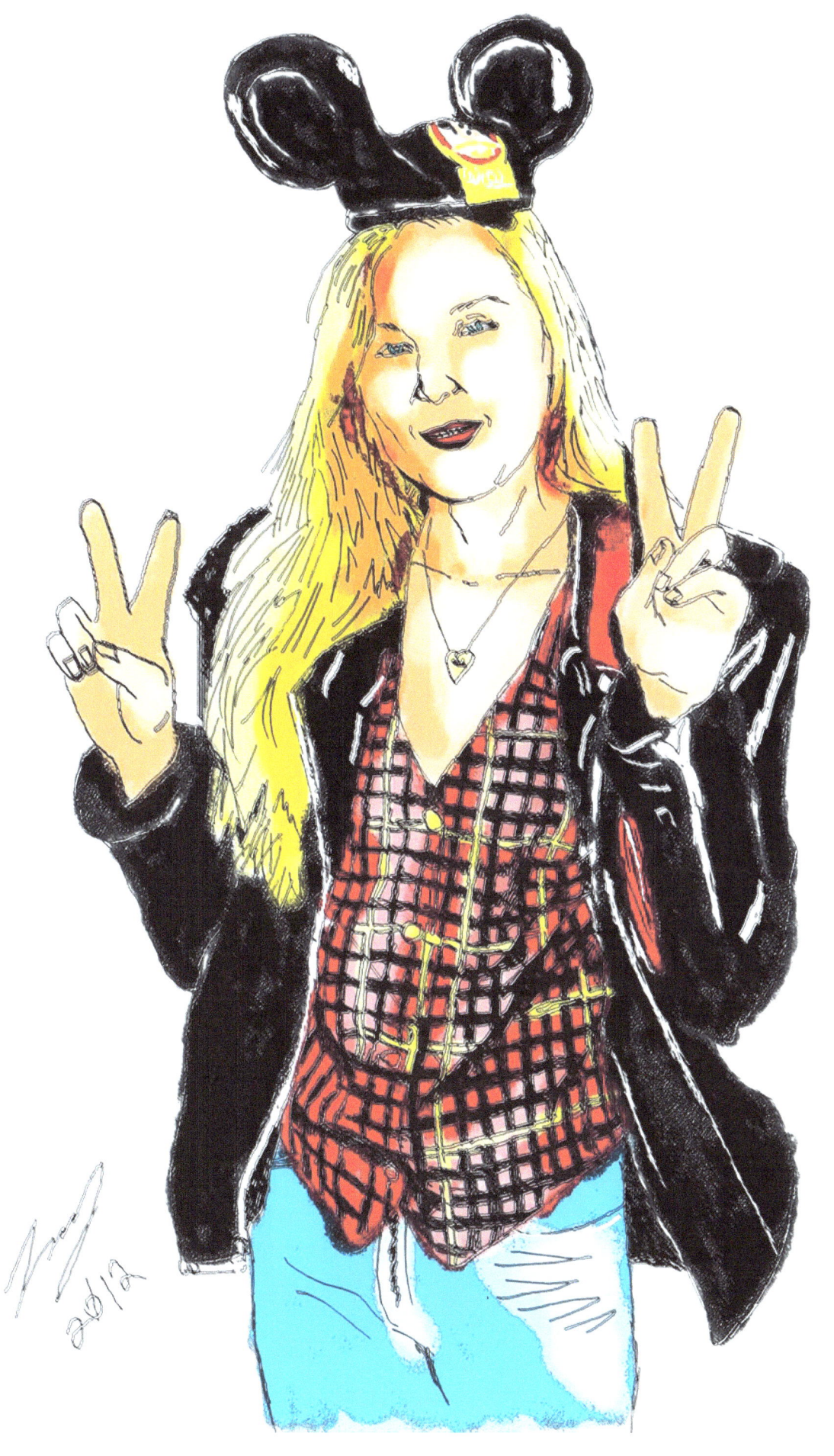

Ilona
By Benjamin Long 2012

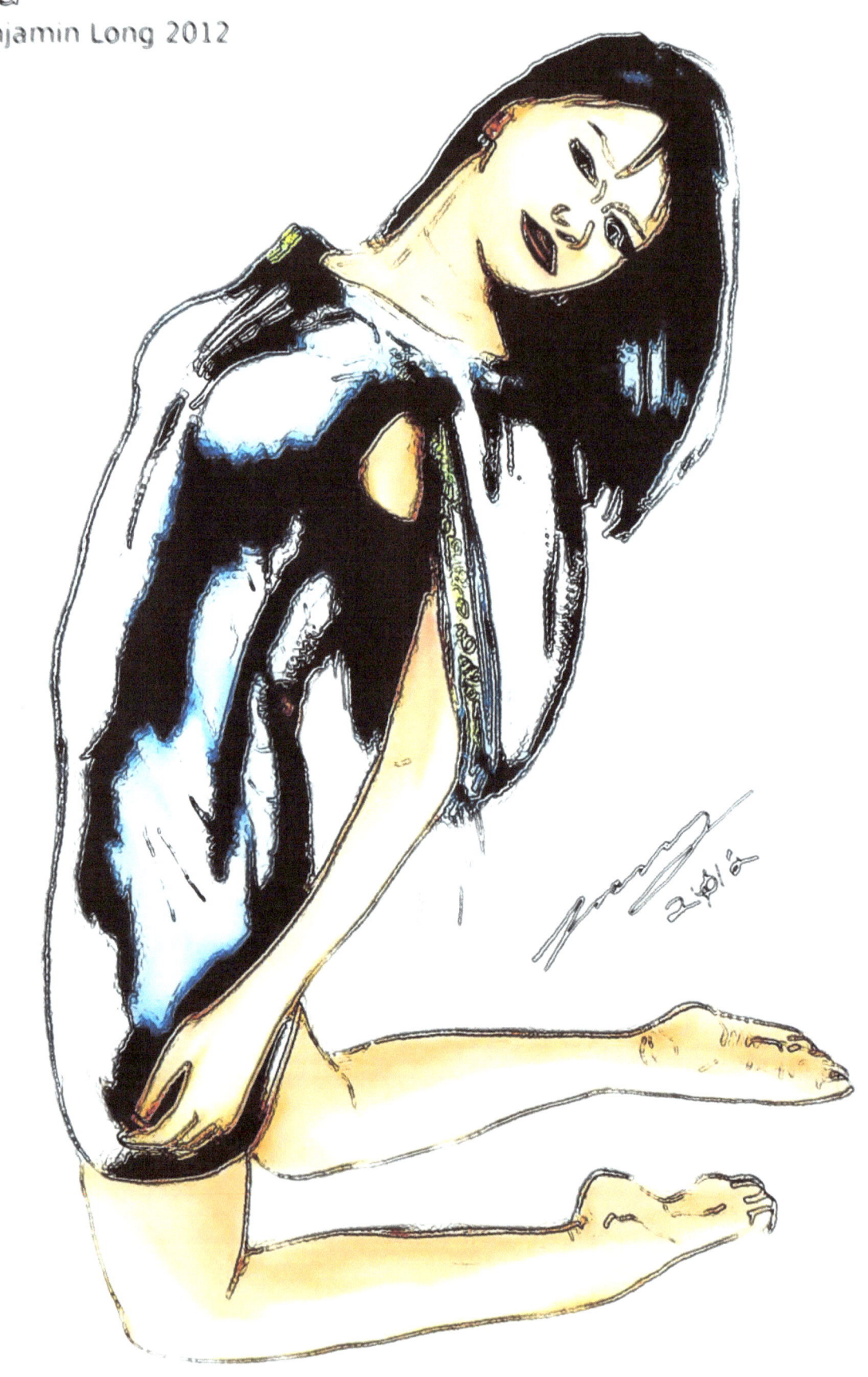

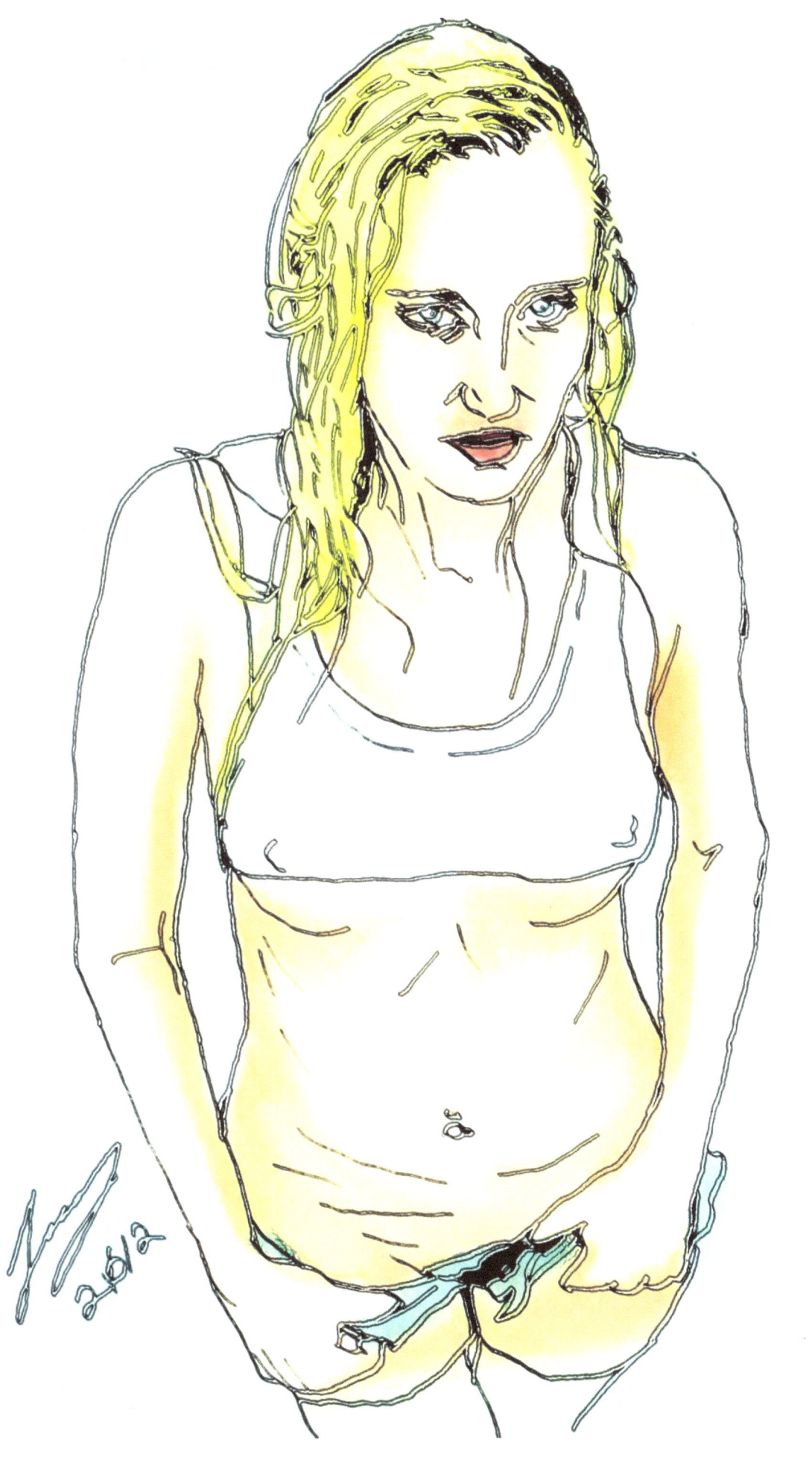

Pregnant Model

Drawing

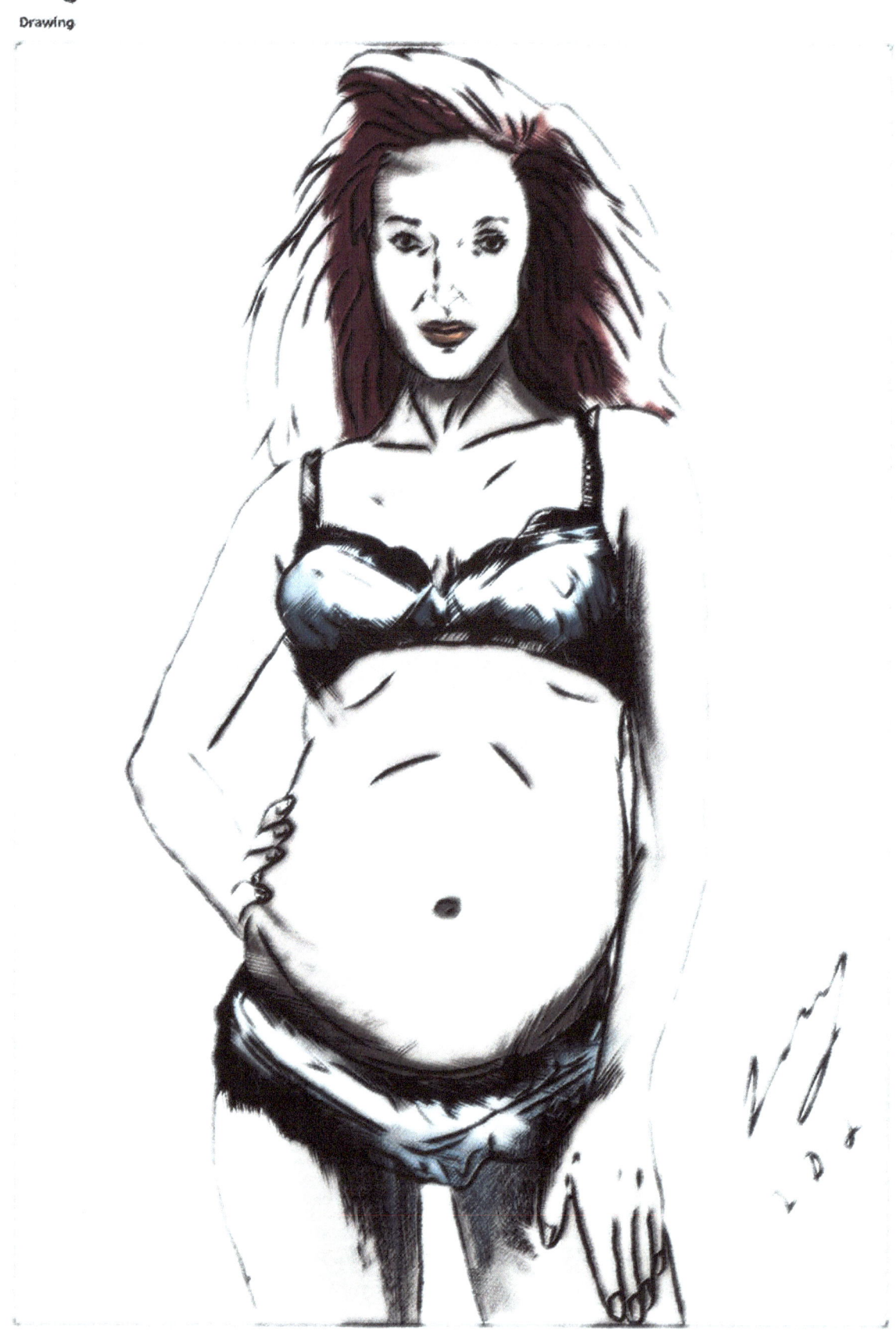

Illustrated by Benjamin Long 2012

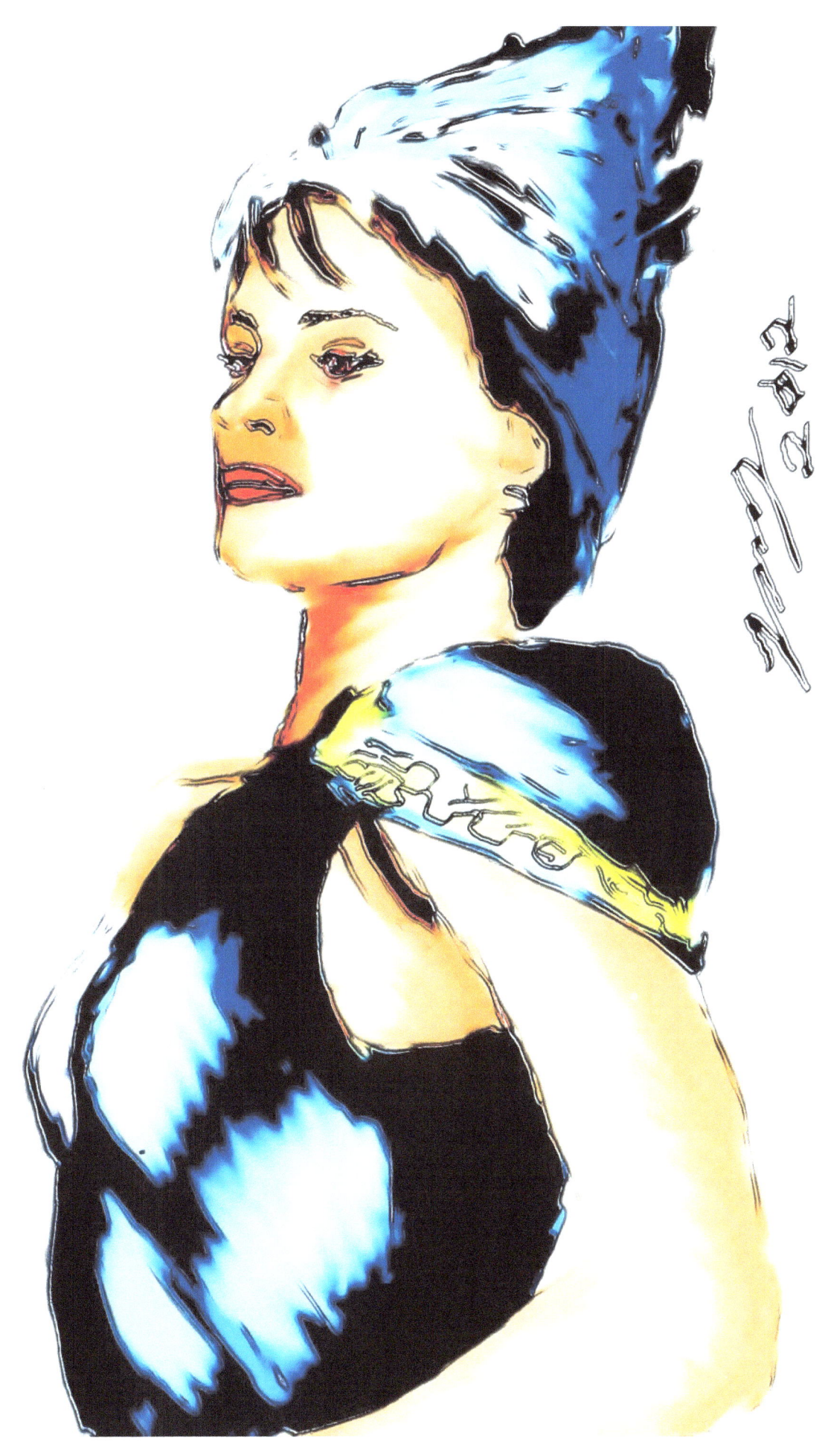

The Doorway

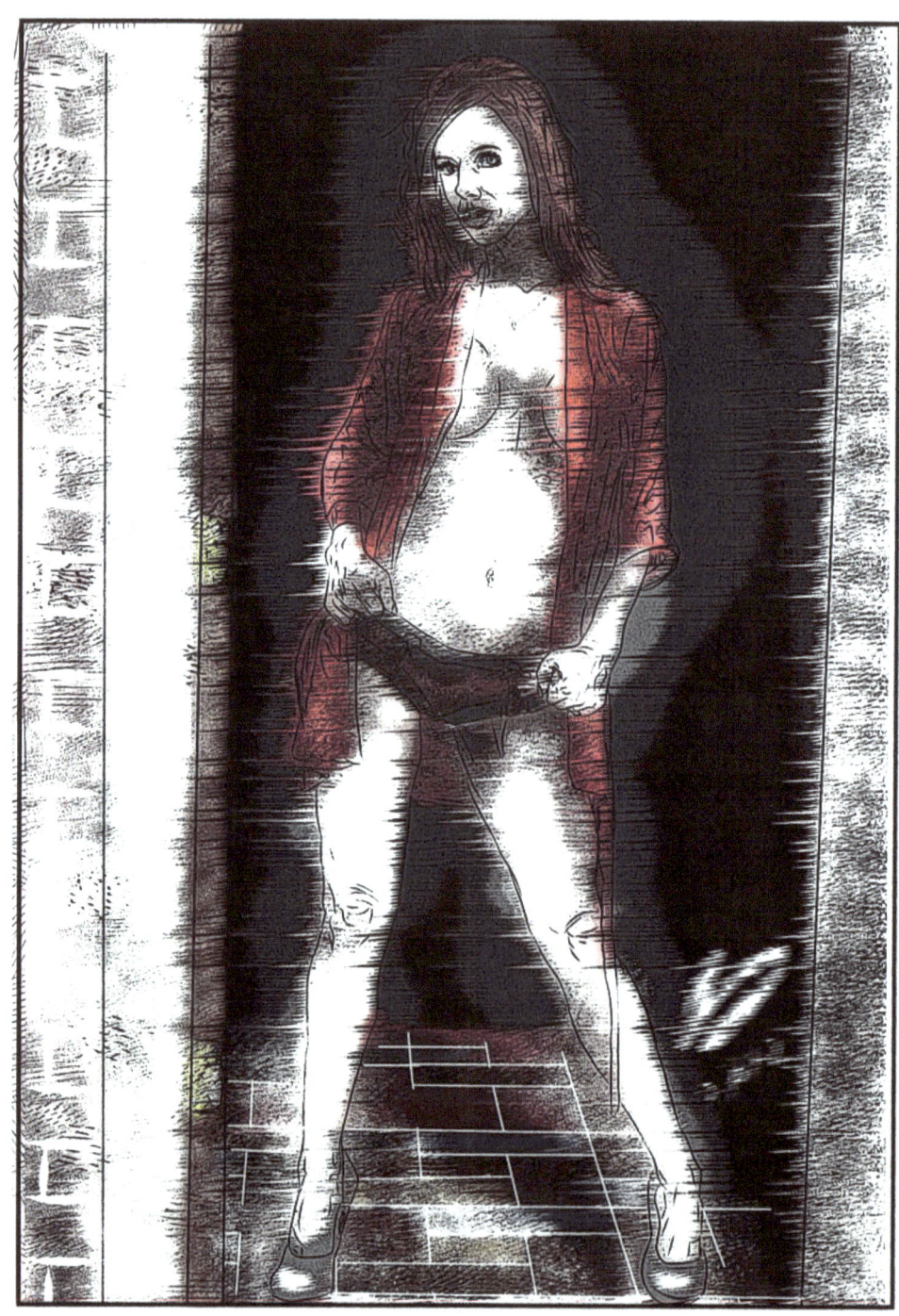

Illustrated by Benjamin Long 2012

Tag der Rache

Illustration of a Woman in Germany from the
Second Great War. Referenced from a photo
uploaded to Deviant Art by DasBlondeBieste
and Illustrated by Benjamin R Long

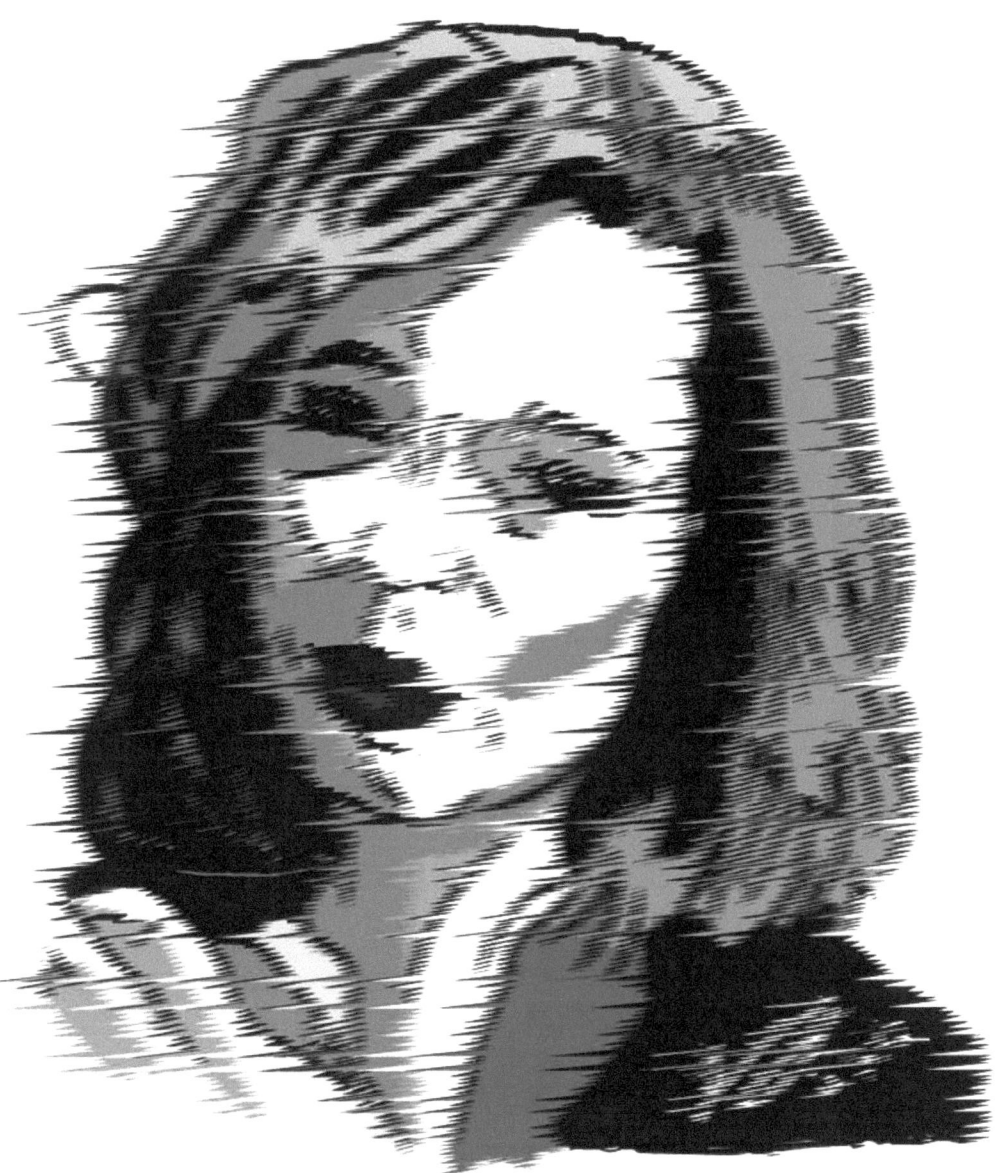

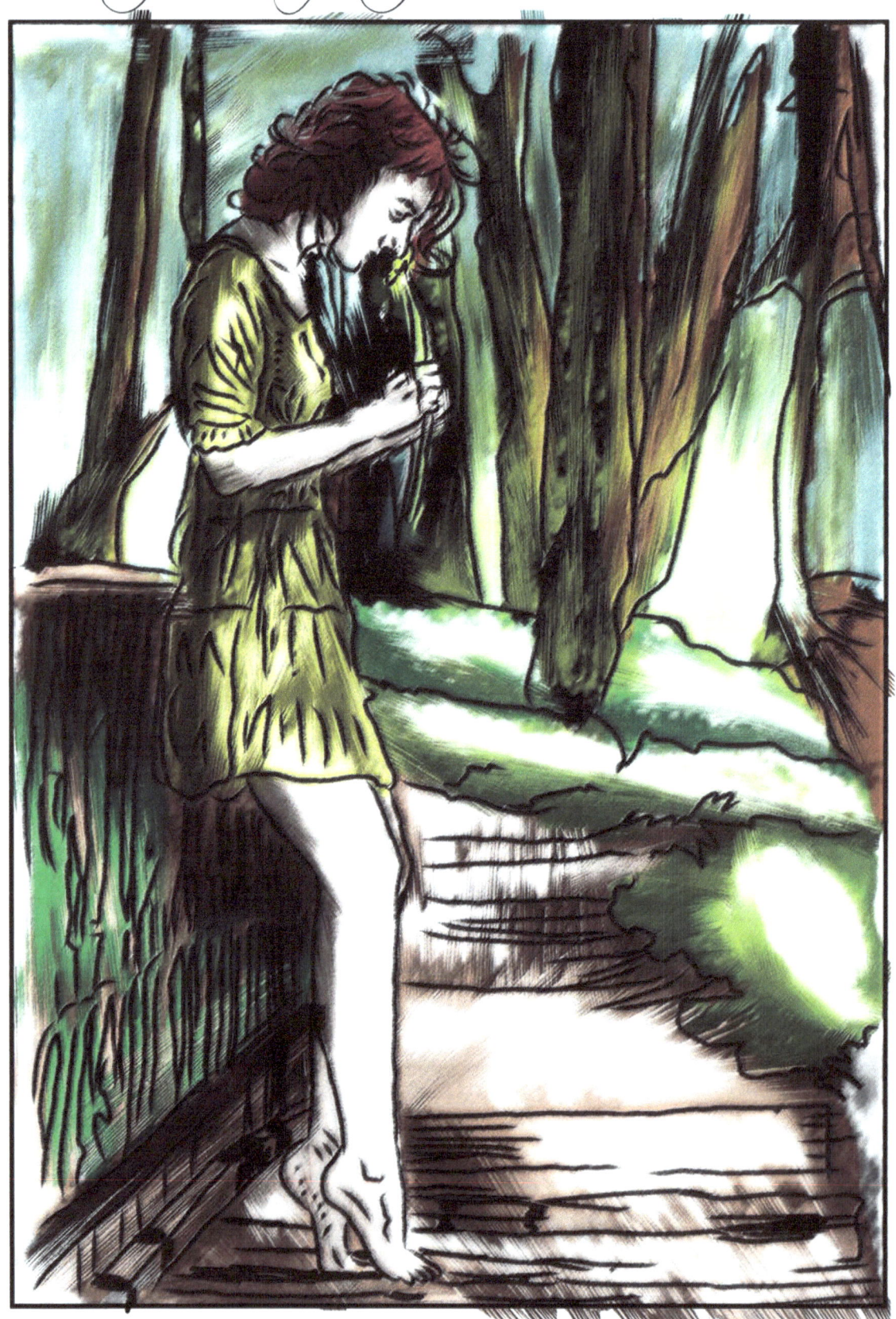

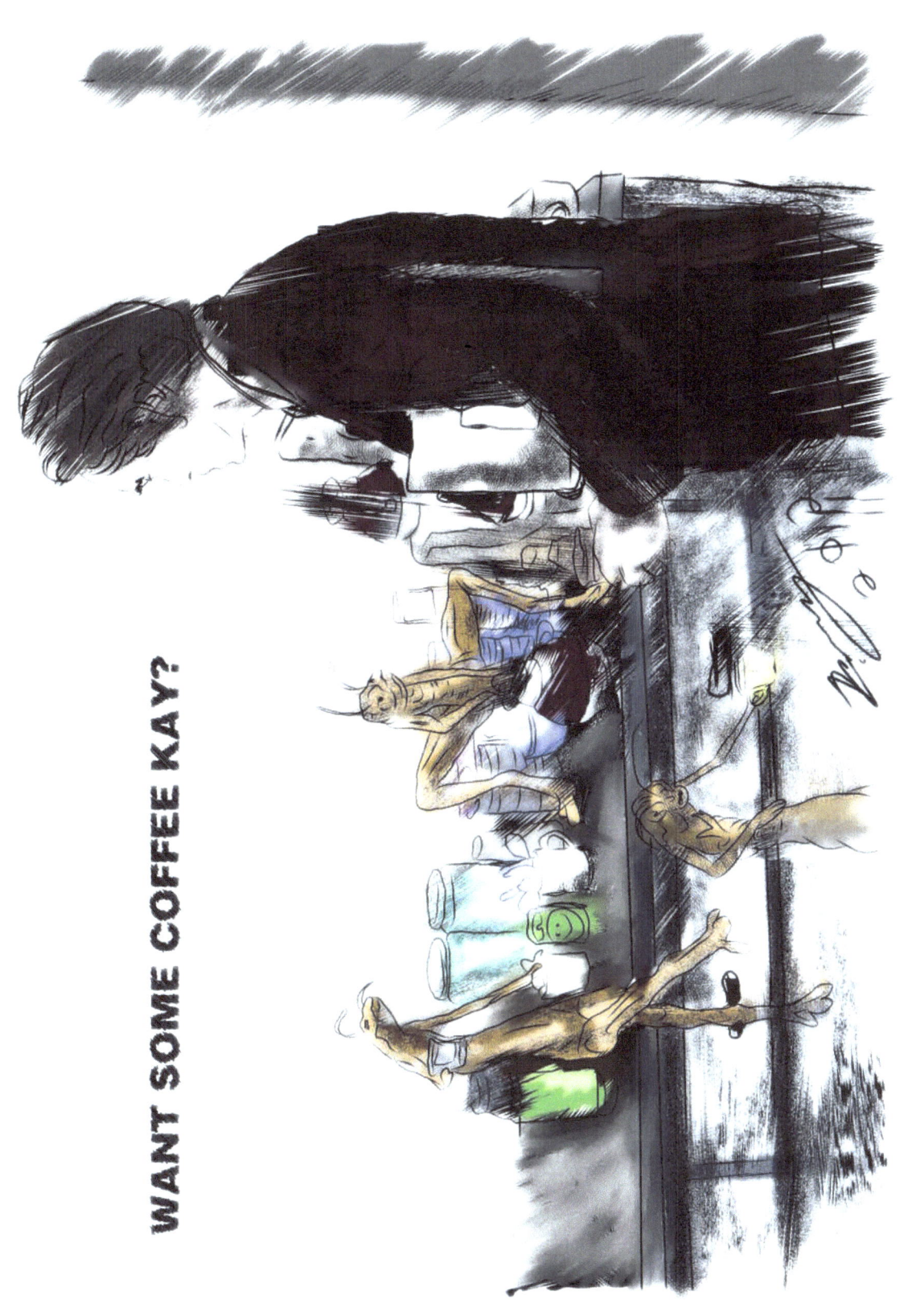

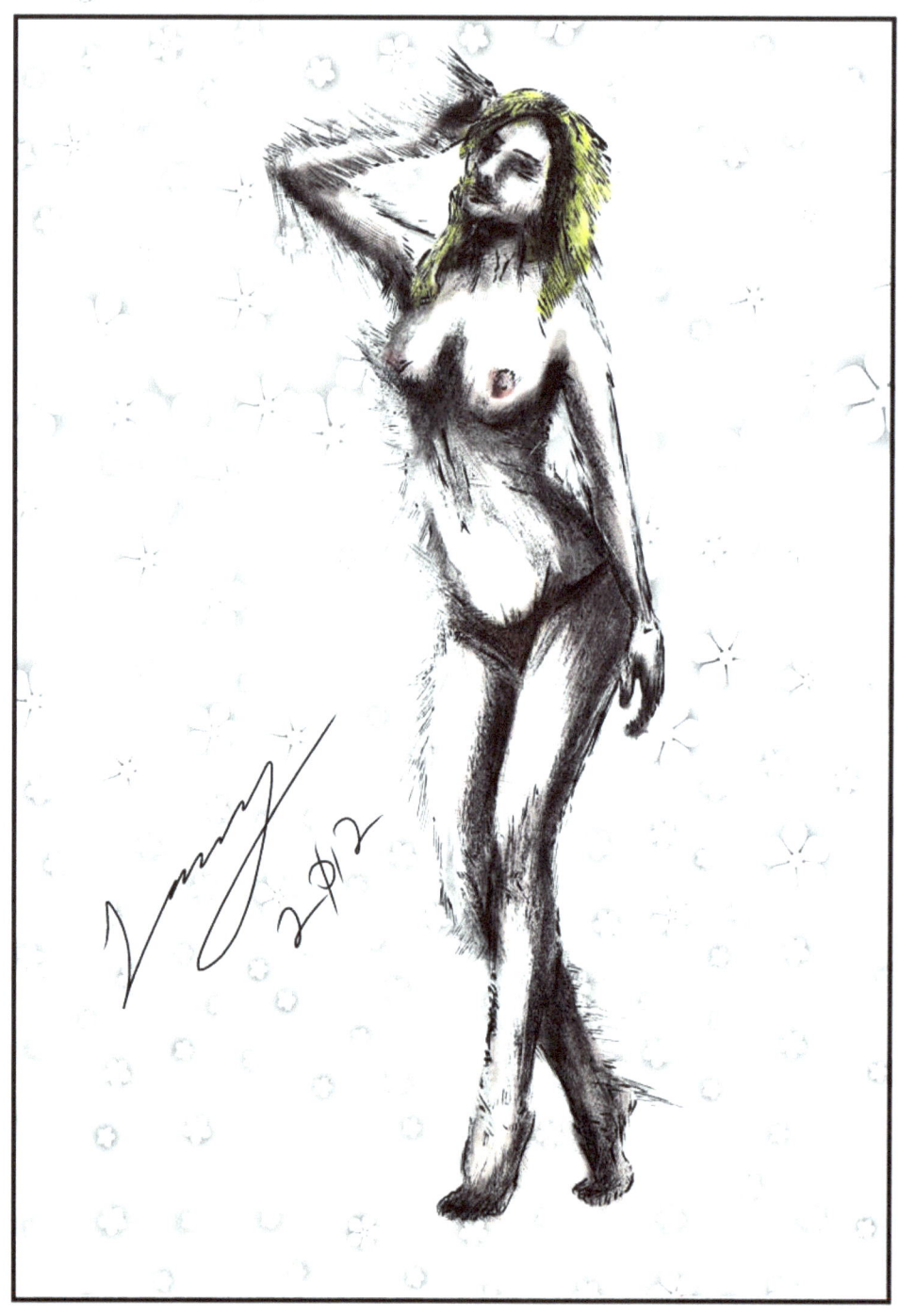

Plat form Heels

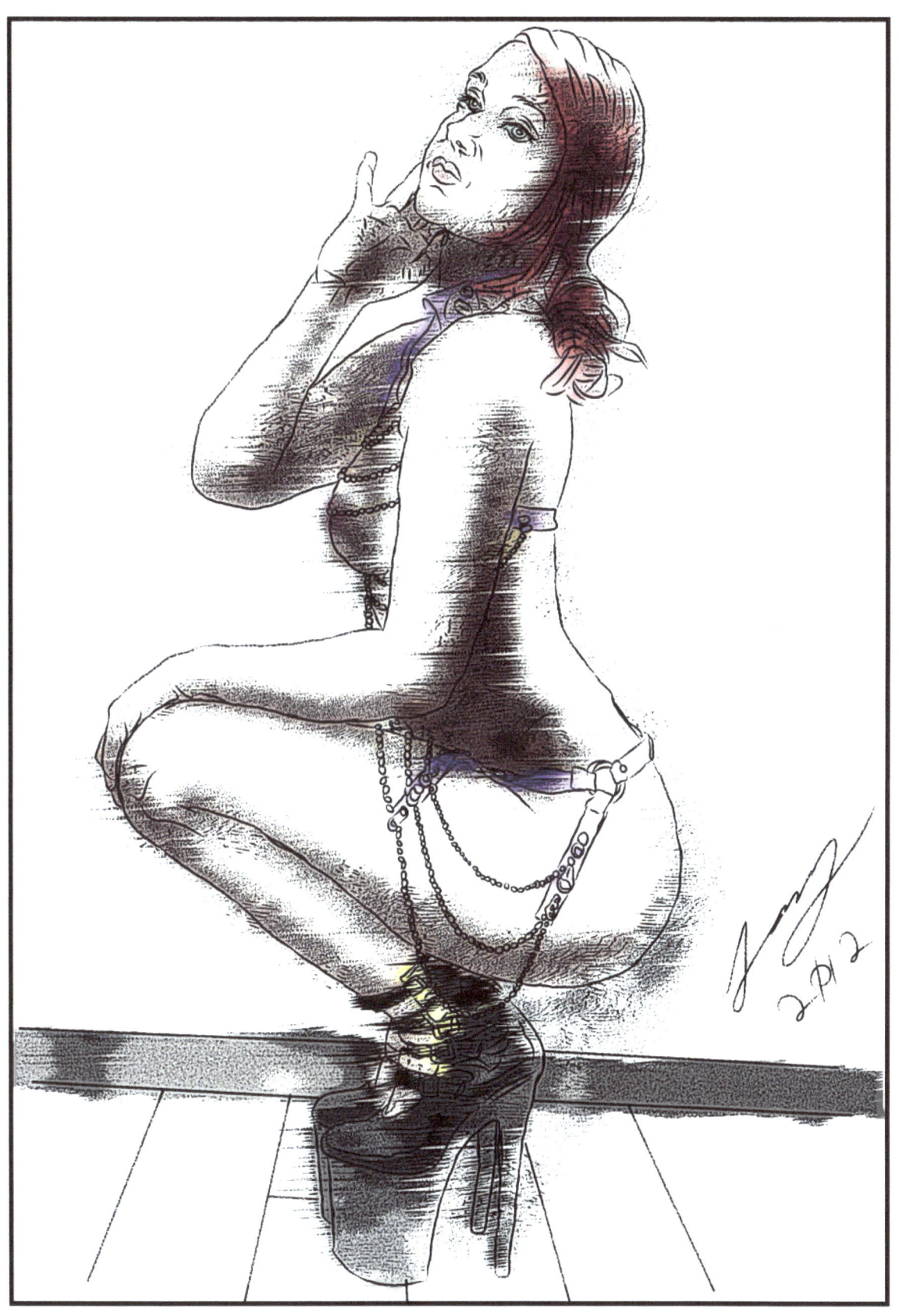

Illustrated by Benjamin R Long 2012

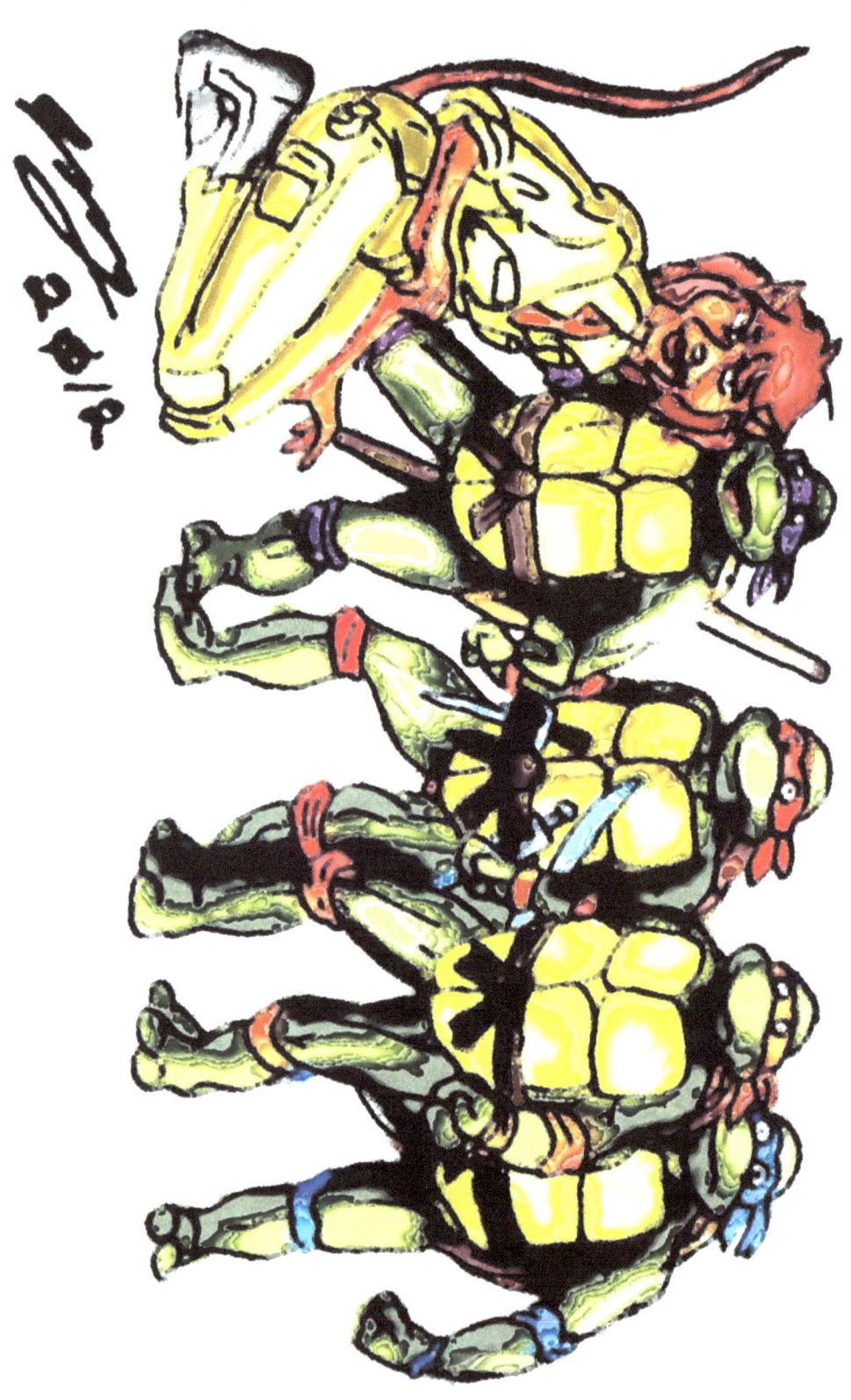

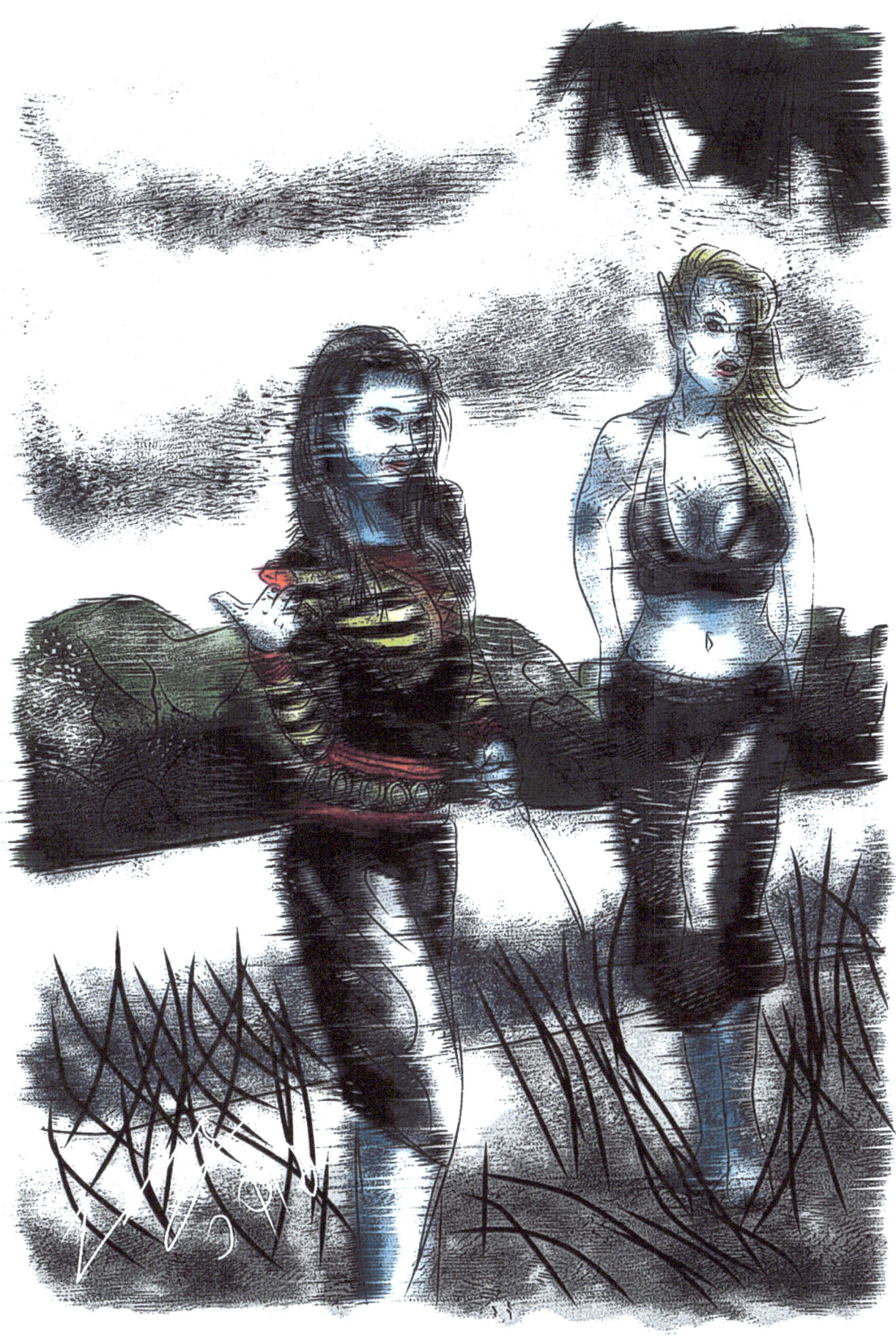

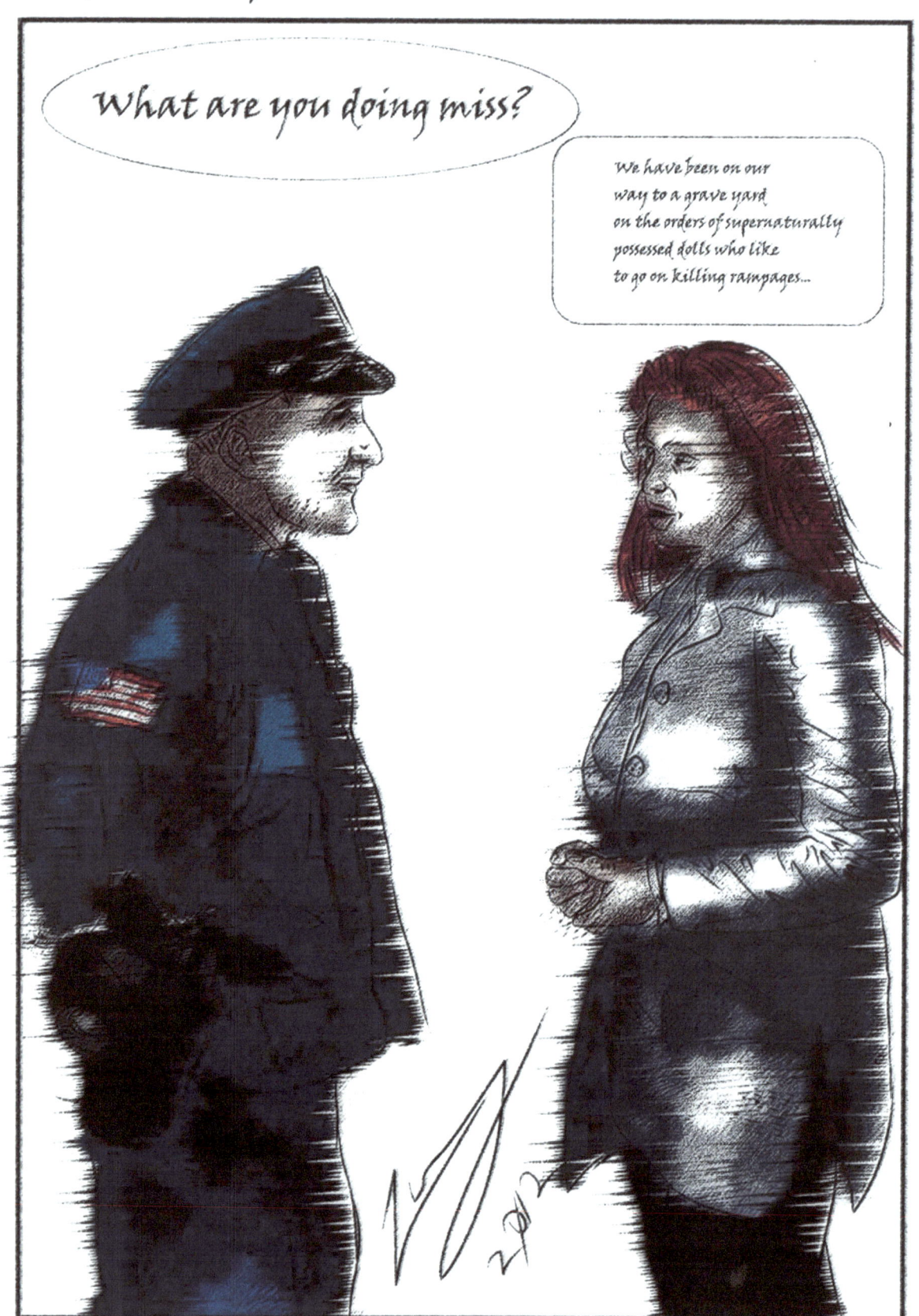

Illustrated by Benjamin Long 2012

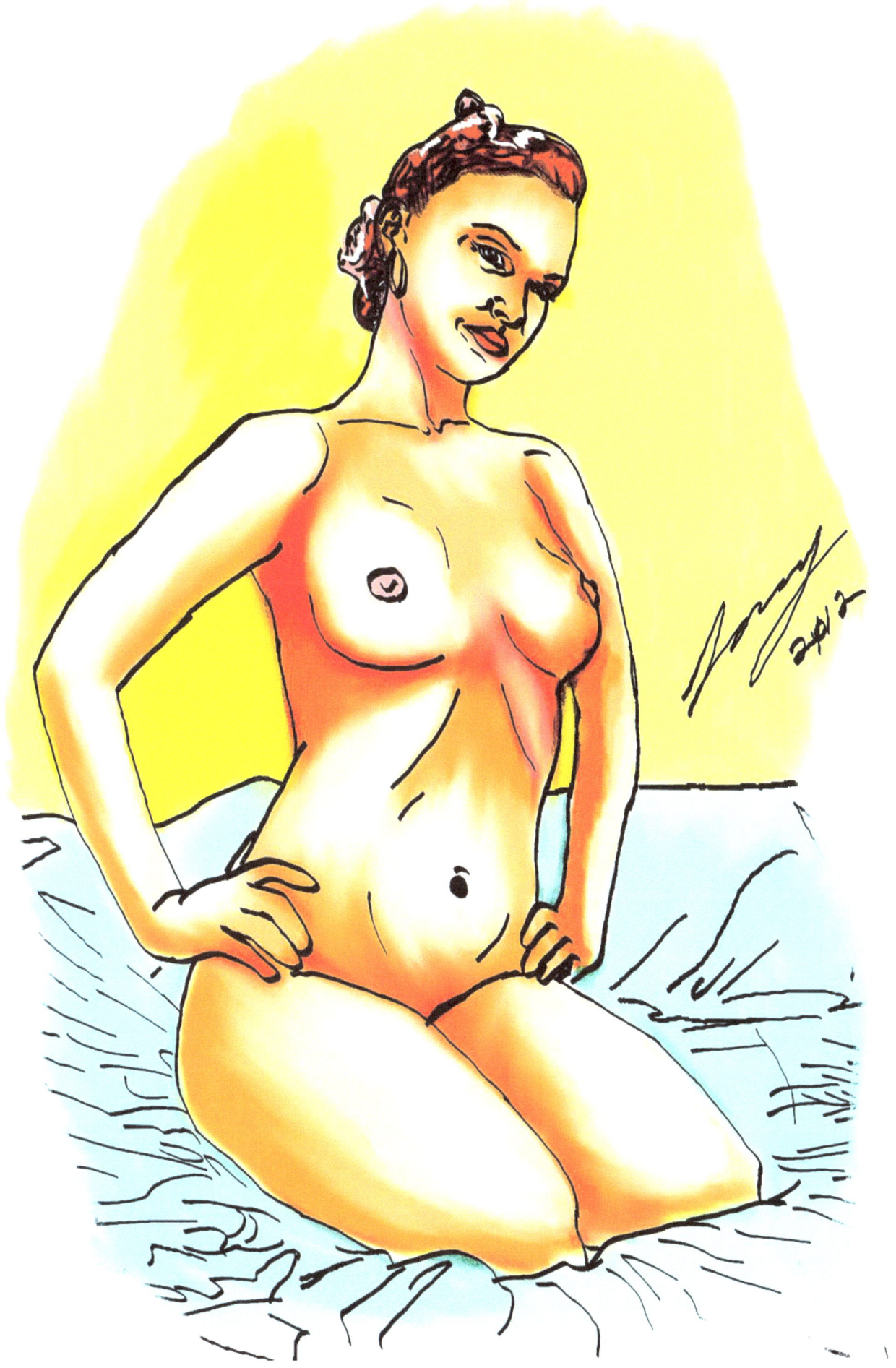

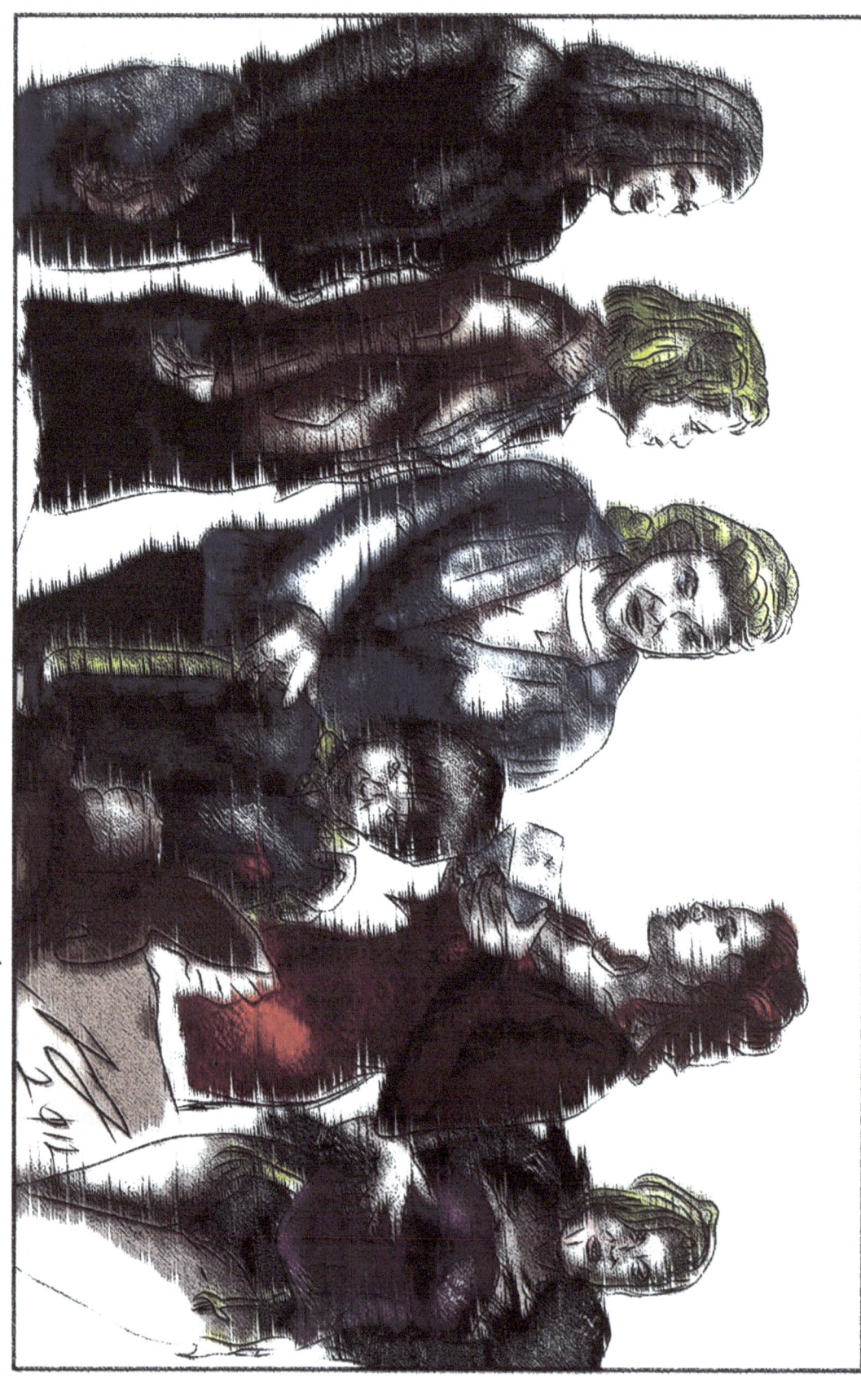

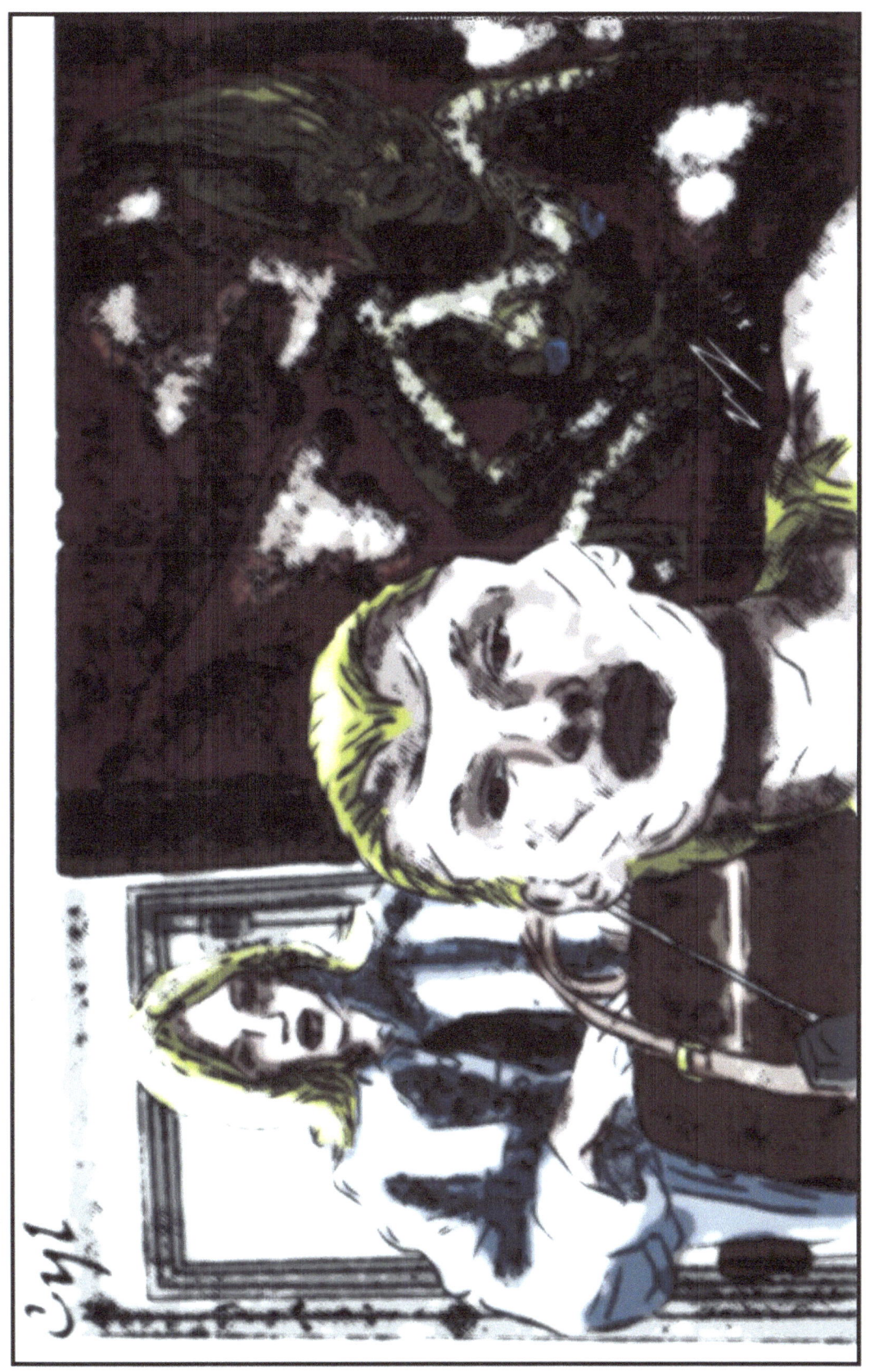

Colt Peacemaker Revolver with Rose Design
By Benjamin Long 2012

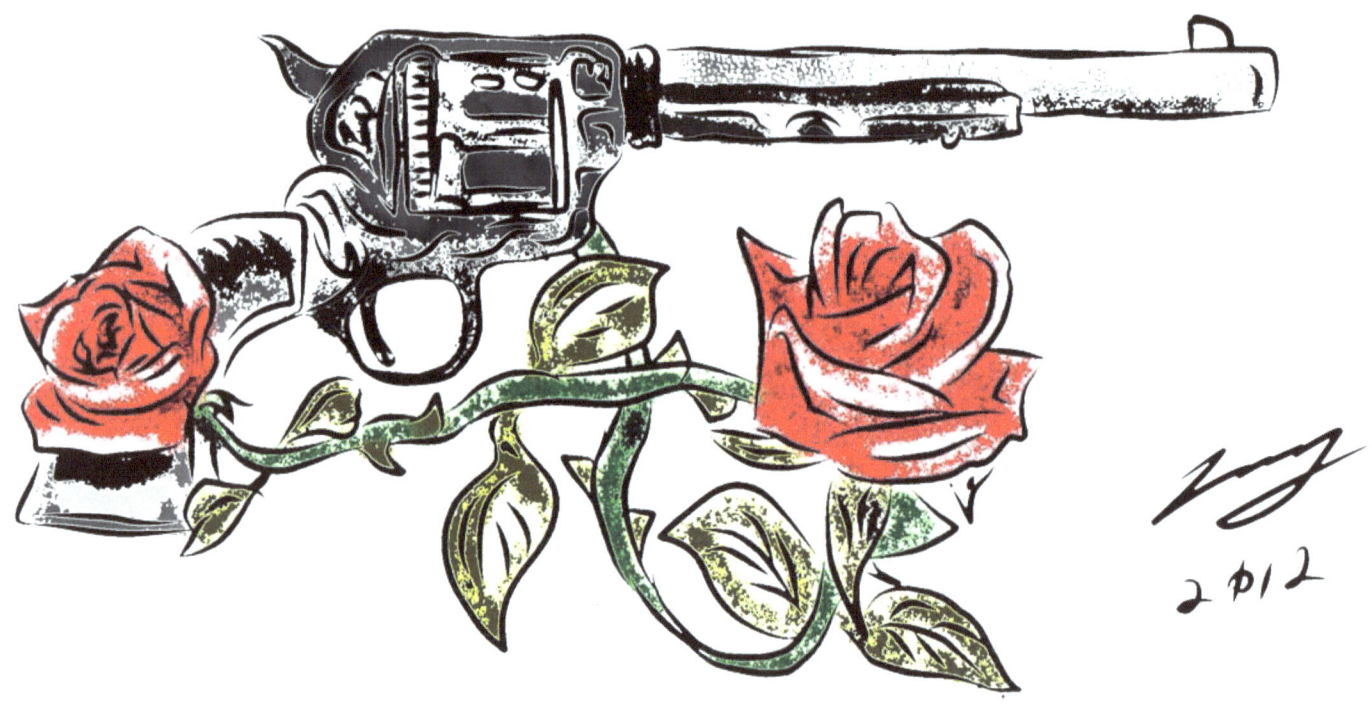

Colt Peacemaker Revolver with Rose Design
By Benjamin Long 2012

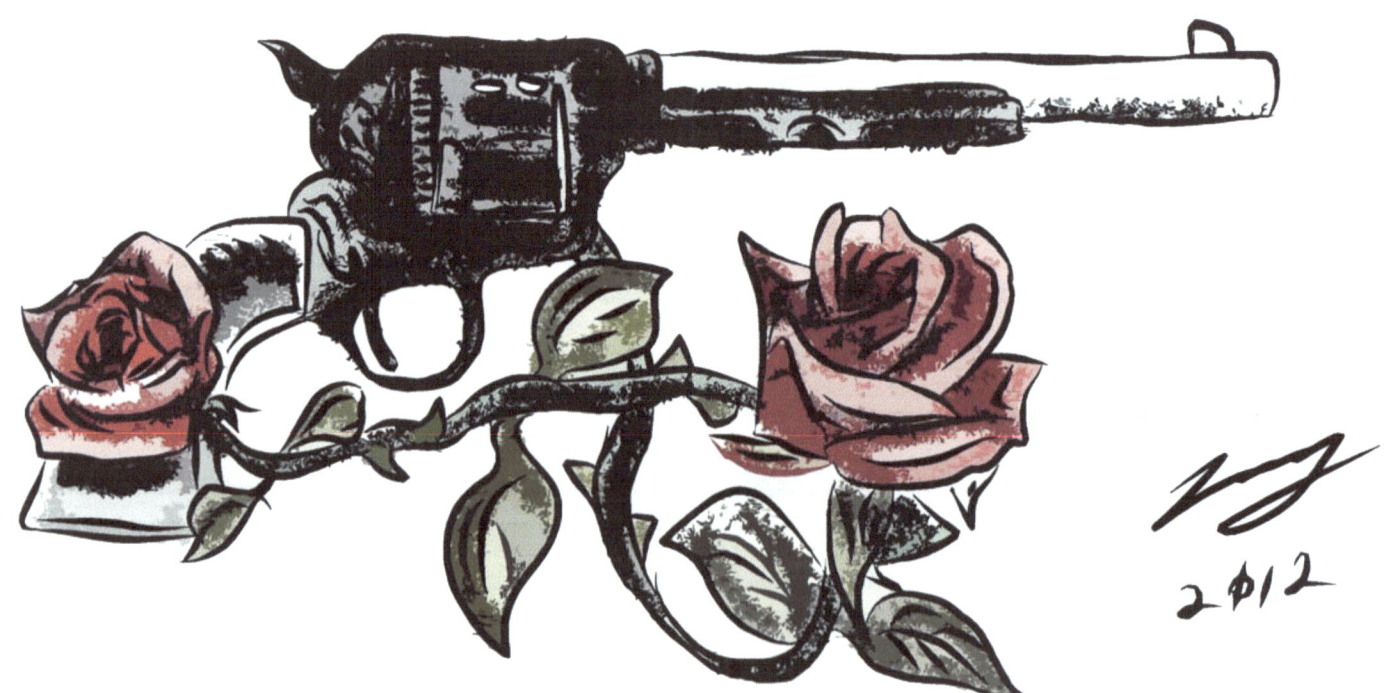

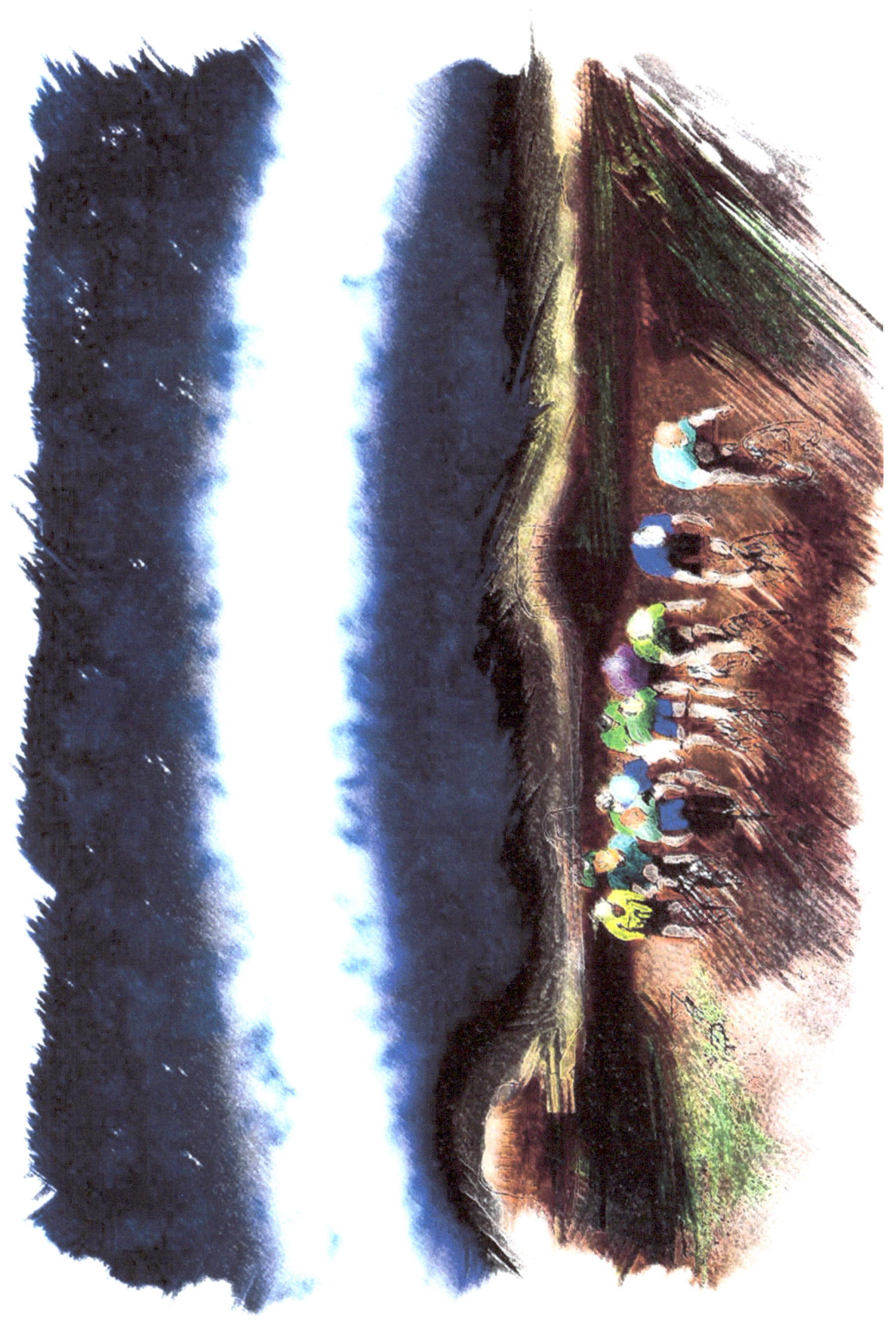

Glowing Woman
By Benjamin Lona 2012.

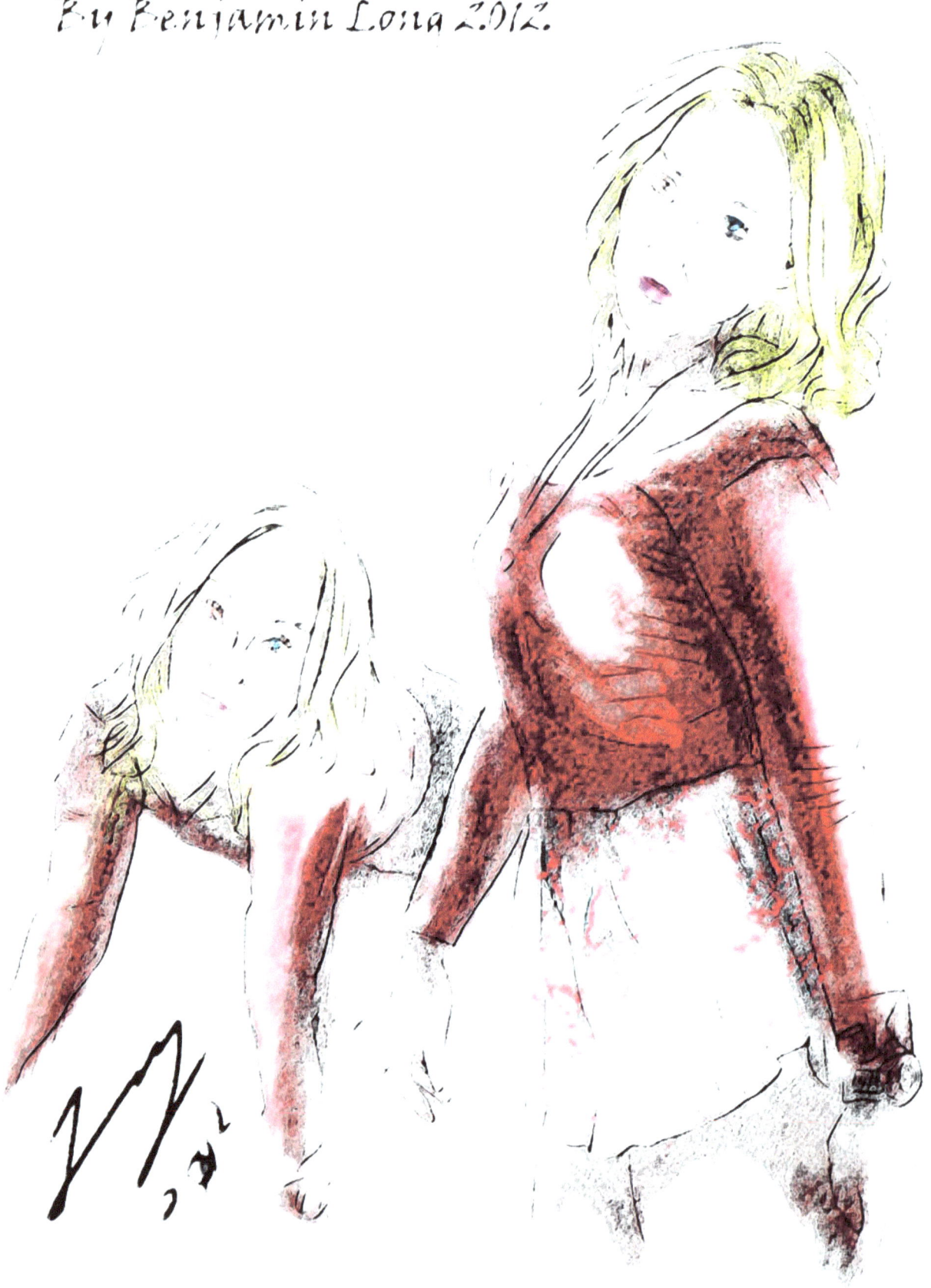

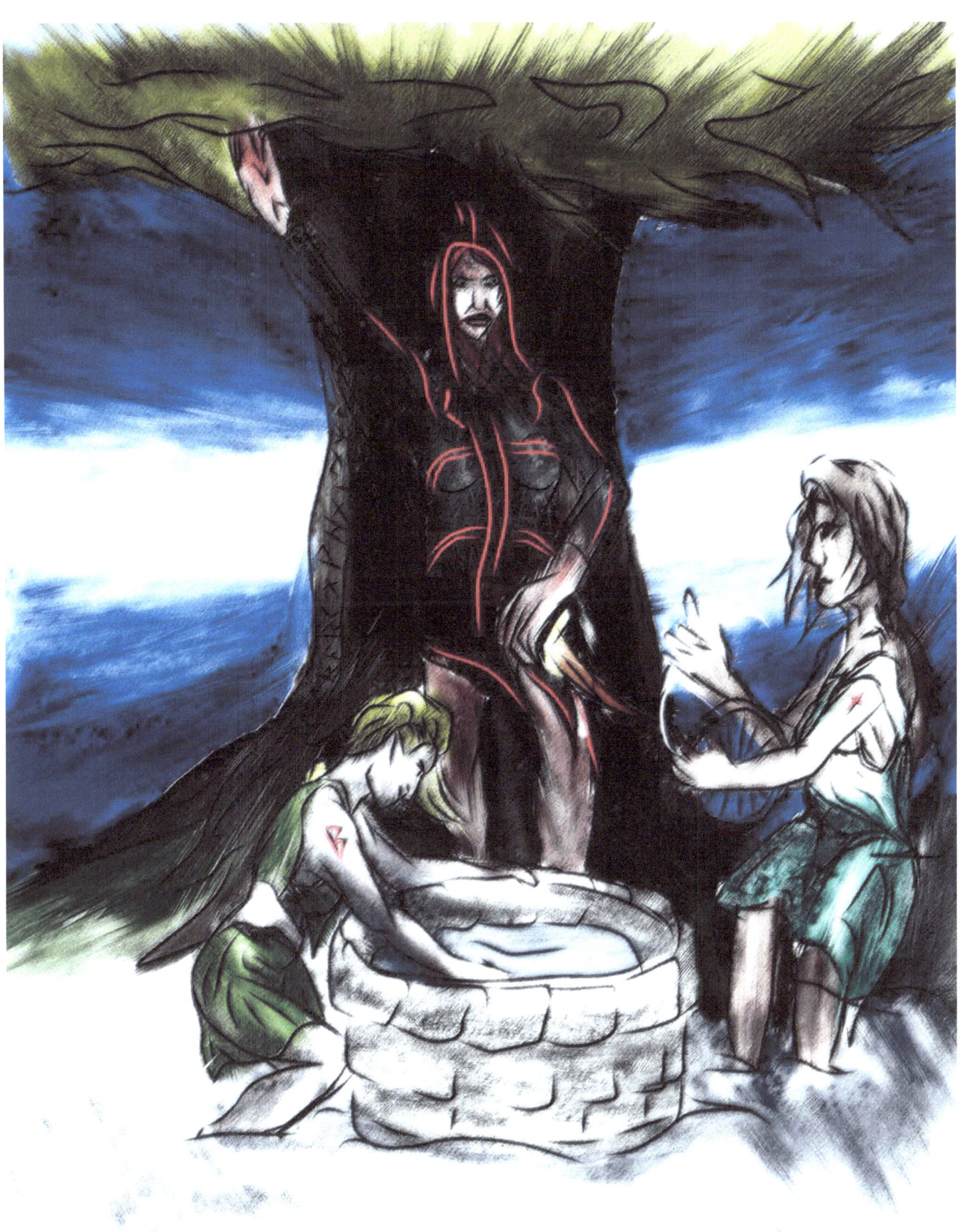

Asian Model

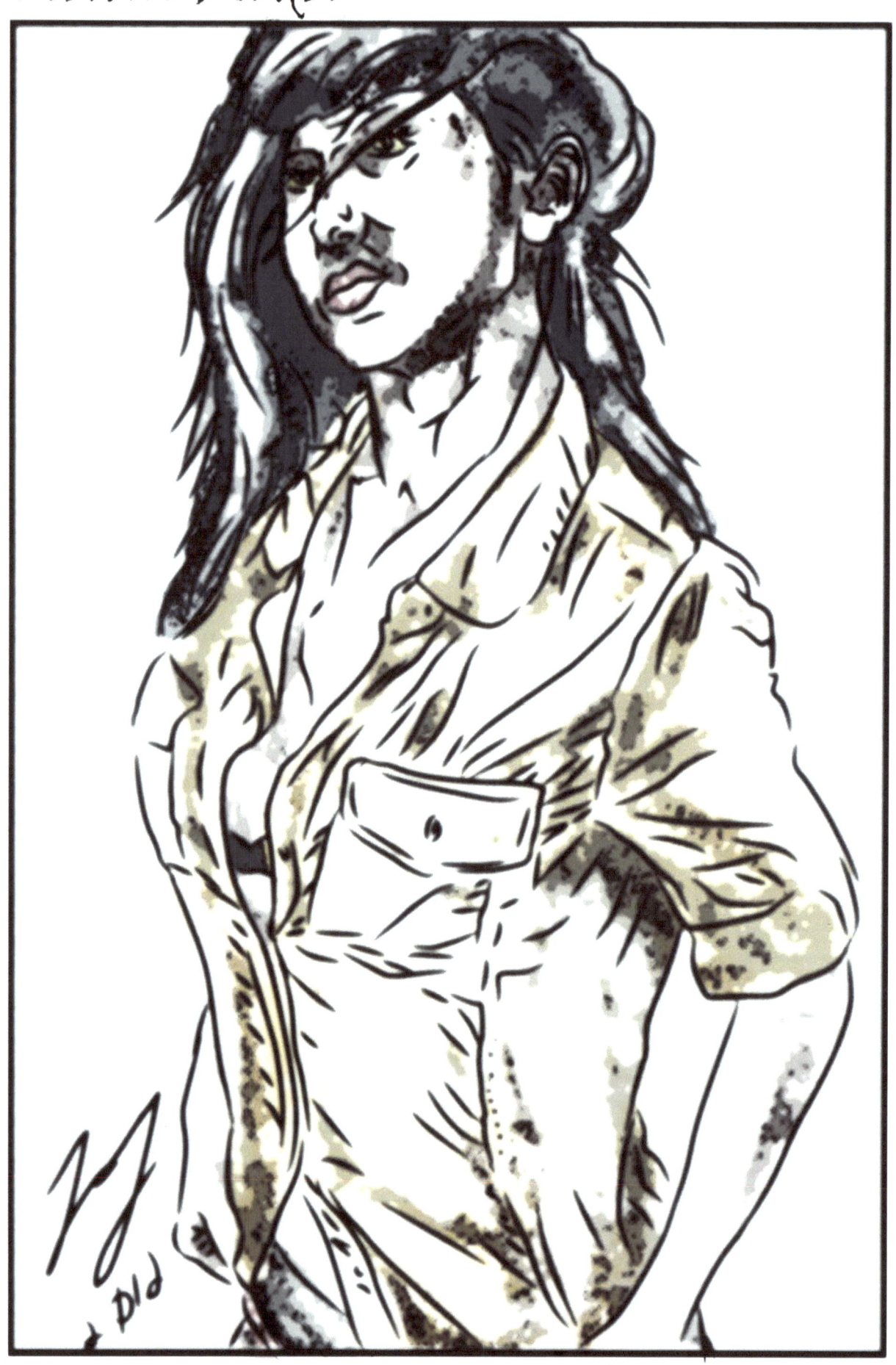

Illustrated by Benjamin Long 2012

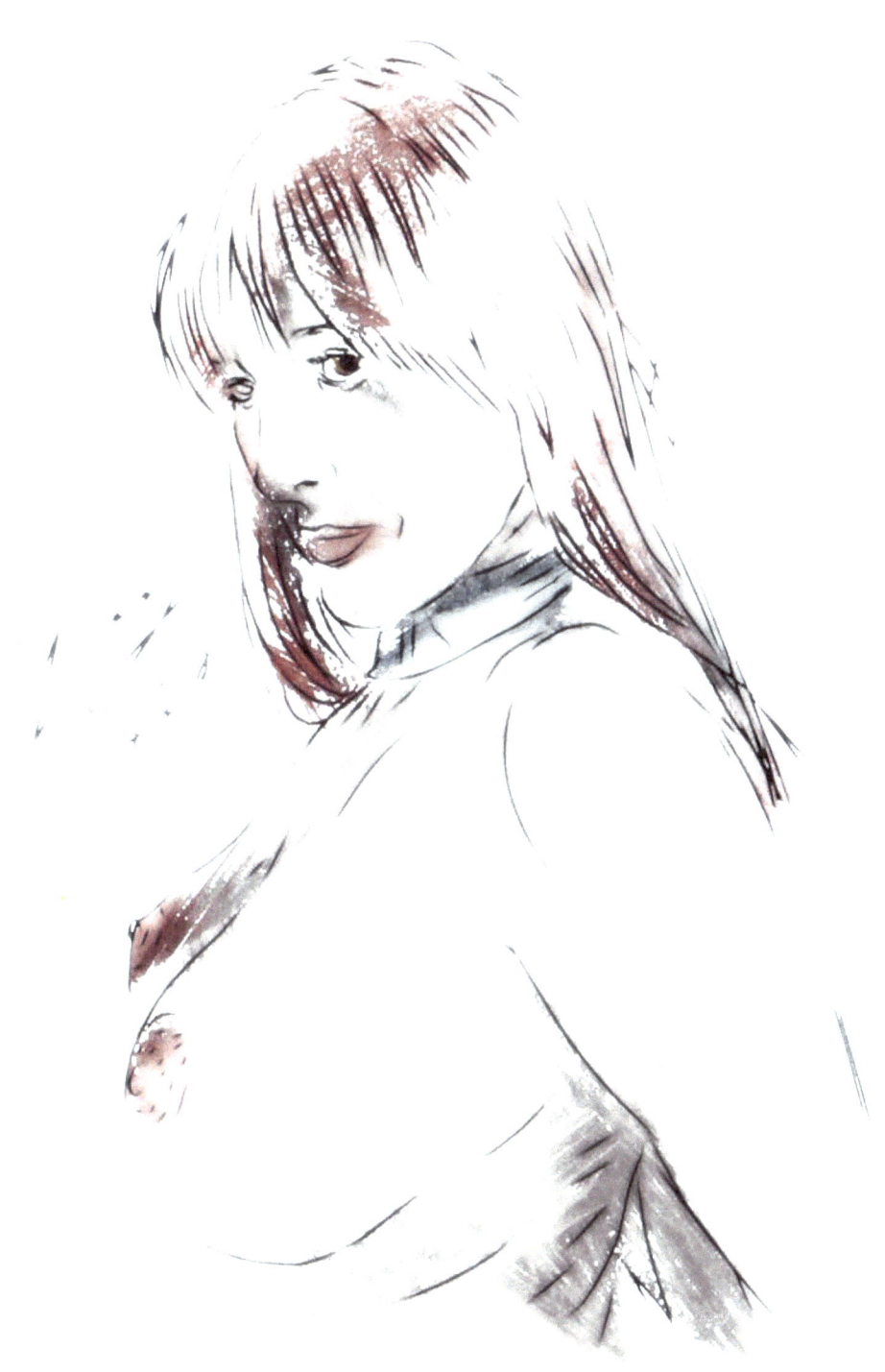

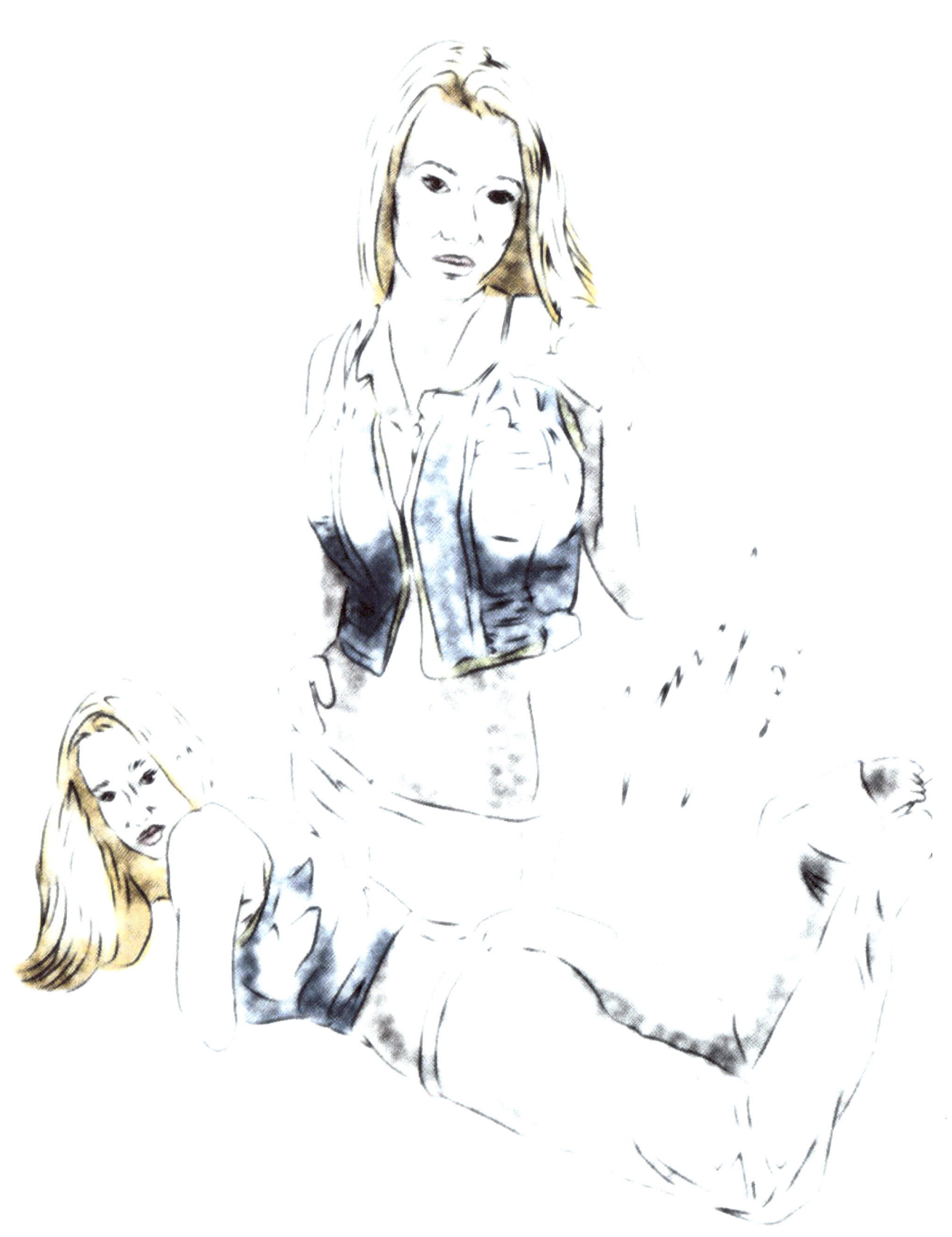

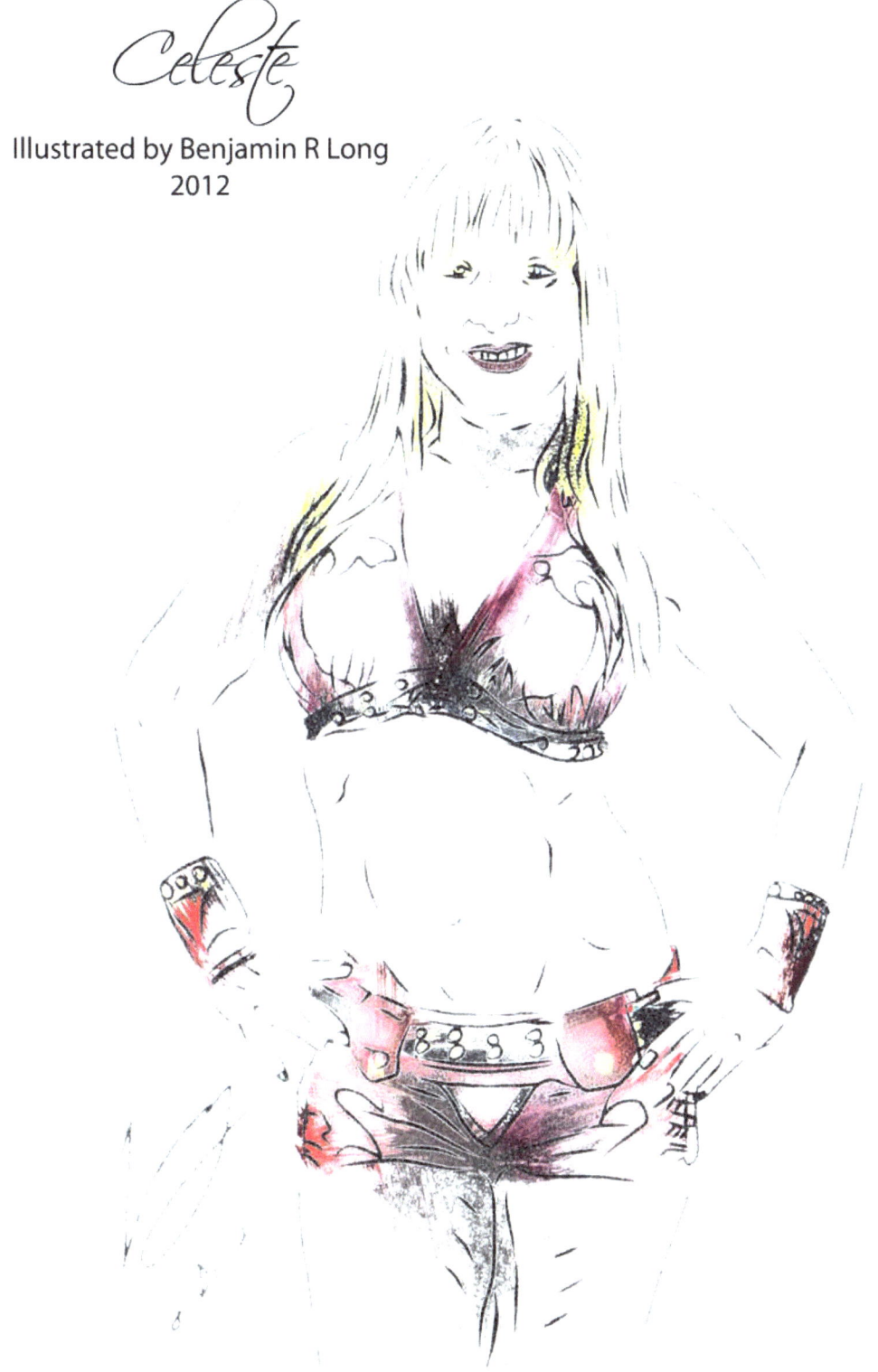

Celeste

Illustrated by Benjamin R Long
2012

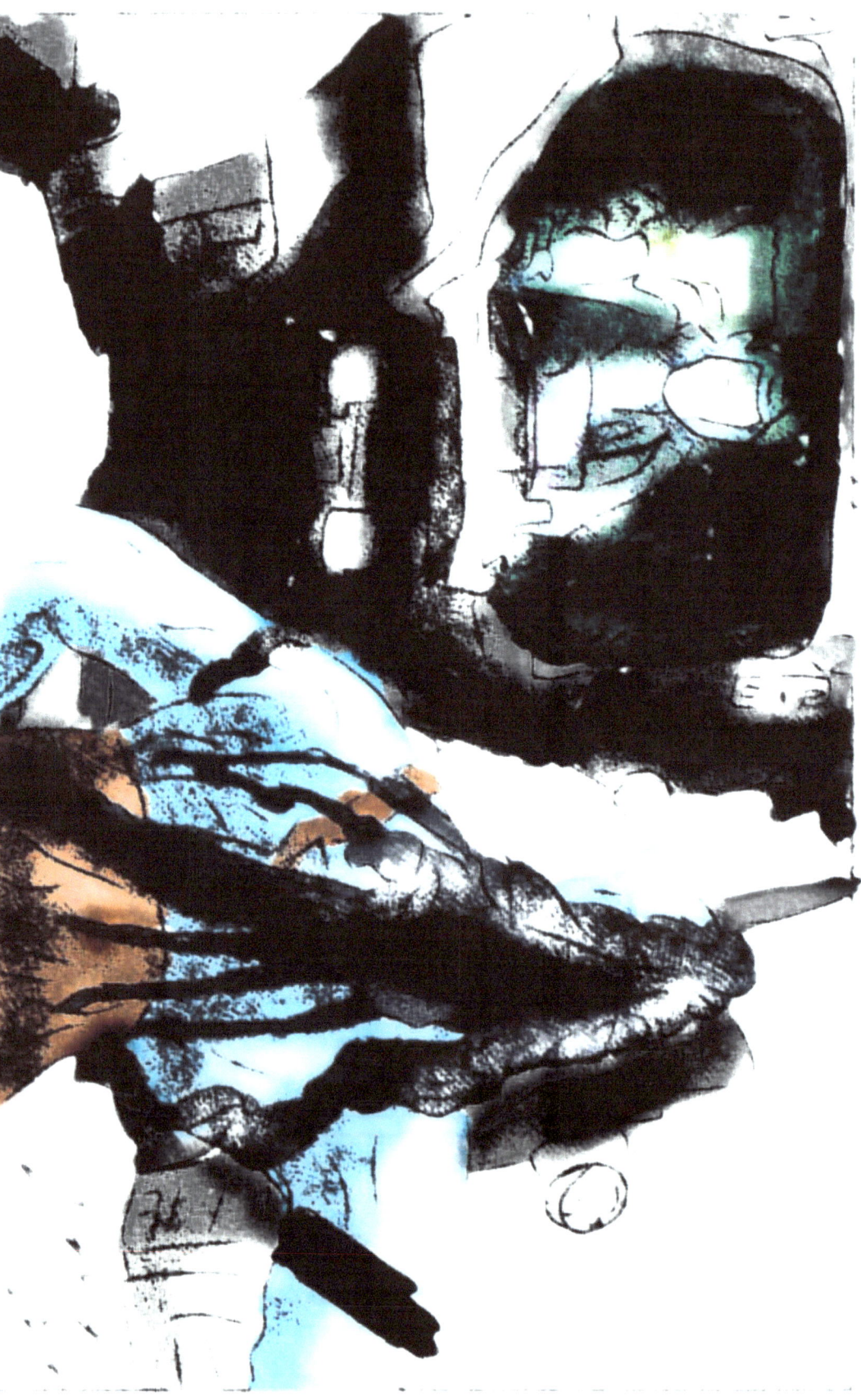

Avatar Standoff

Illustrated by Benjamin Long 2012

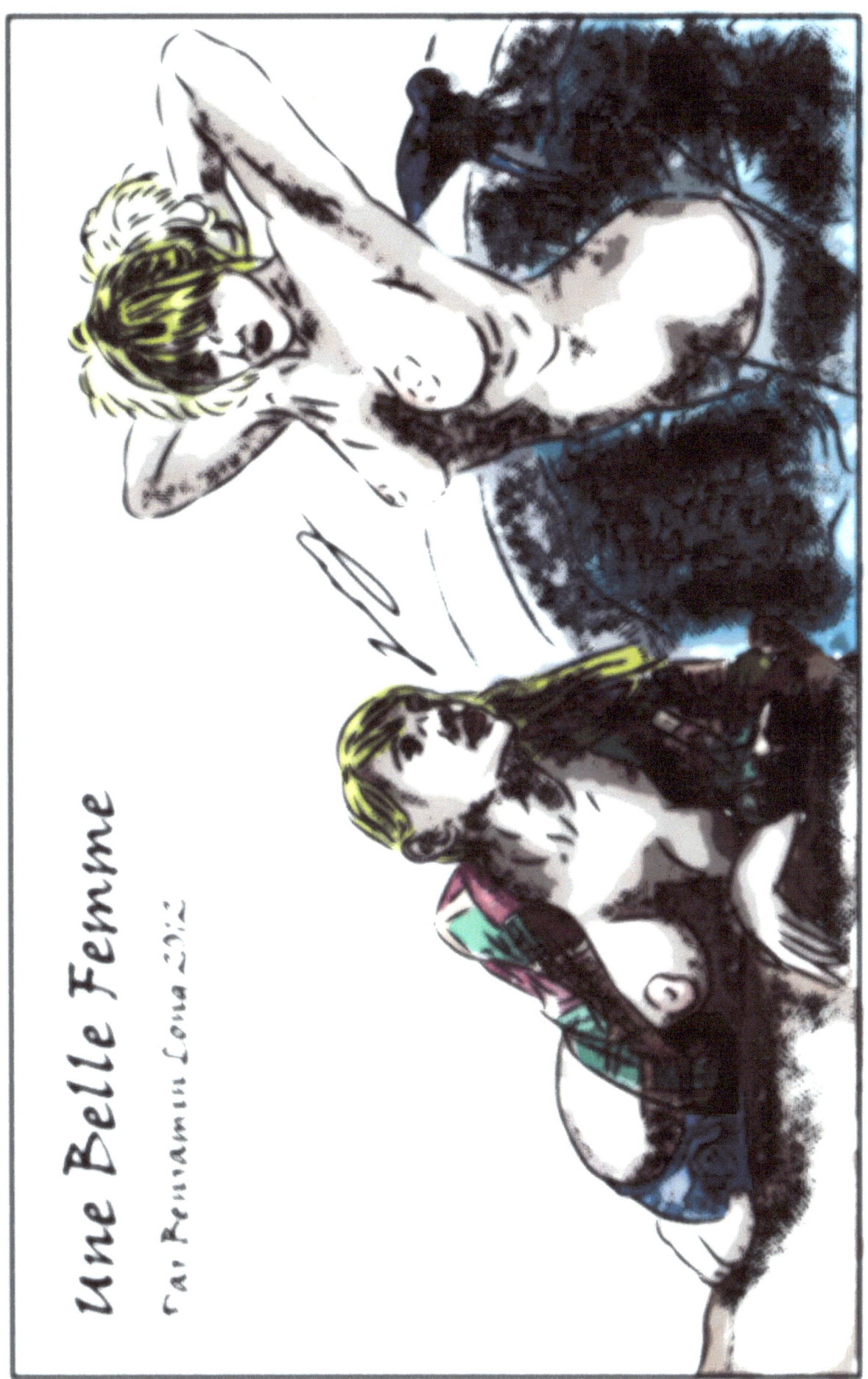

Une Belle Femme

par Benjamin Loua 2012

Black Fin Cat Fish

By Benjamin Long 2012

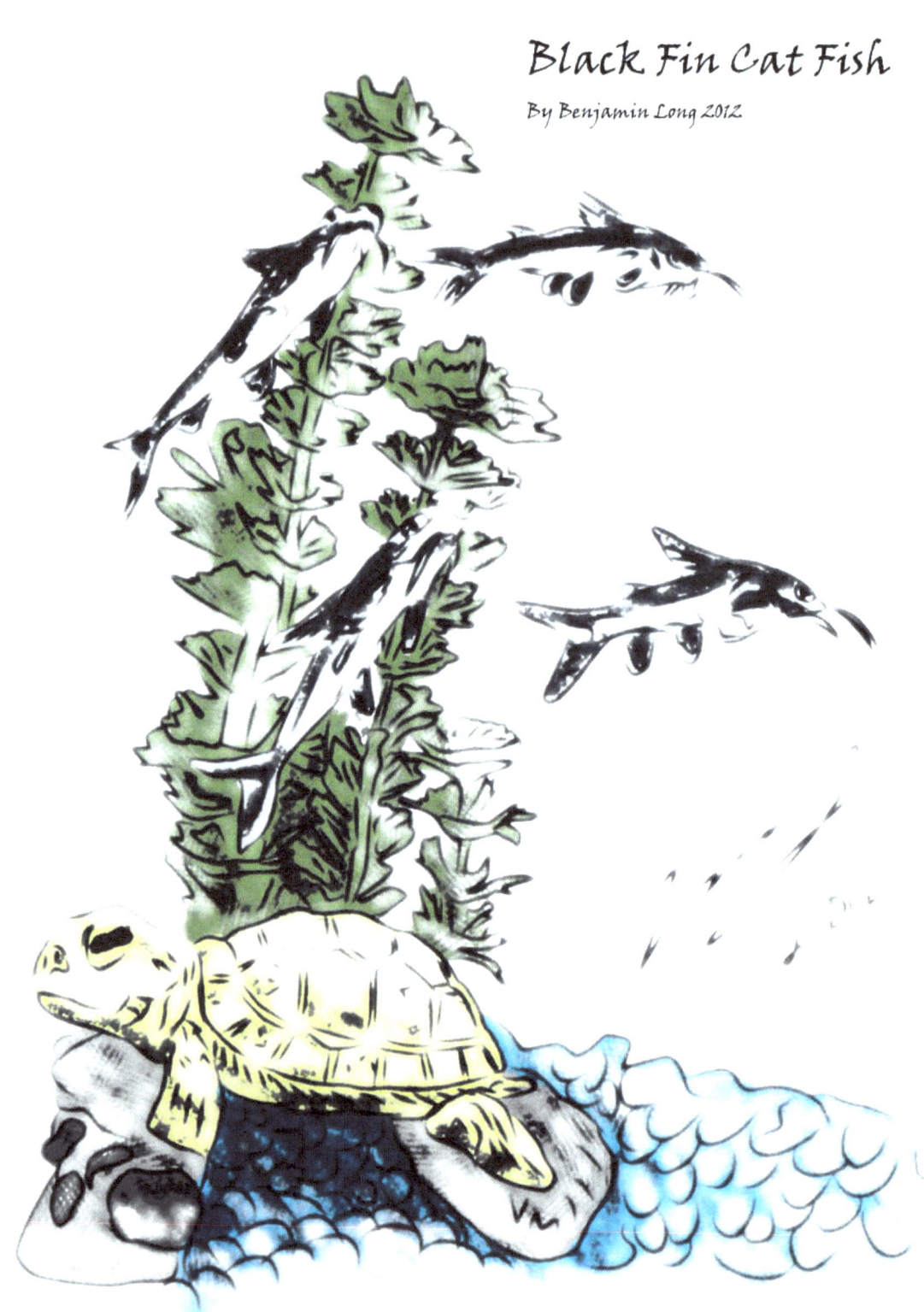

Callie
Ugly Americans

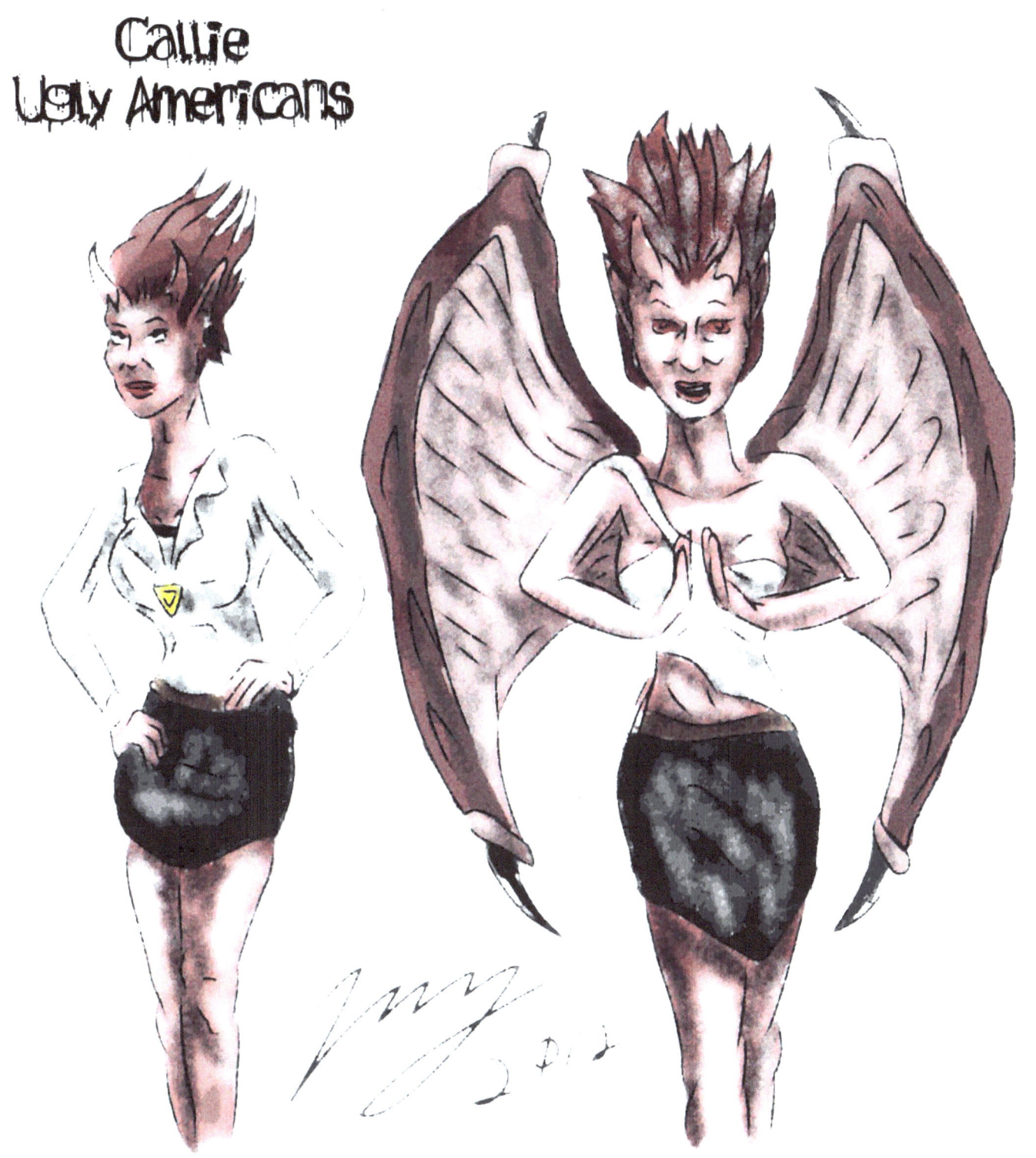

Fairy Christina - Woodland Fairy

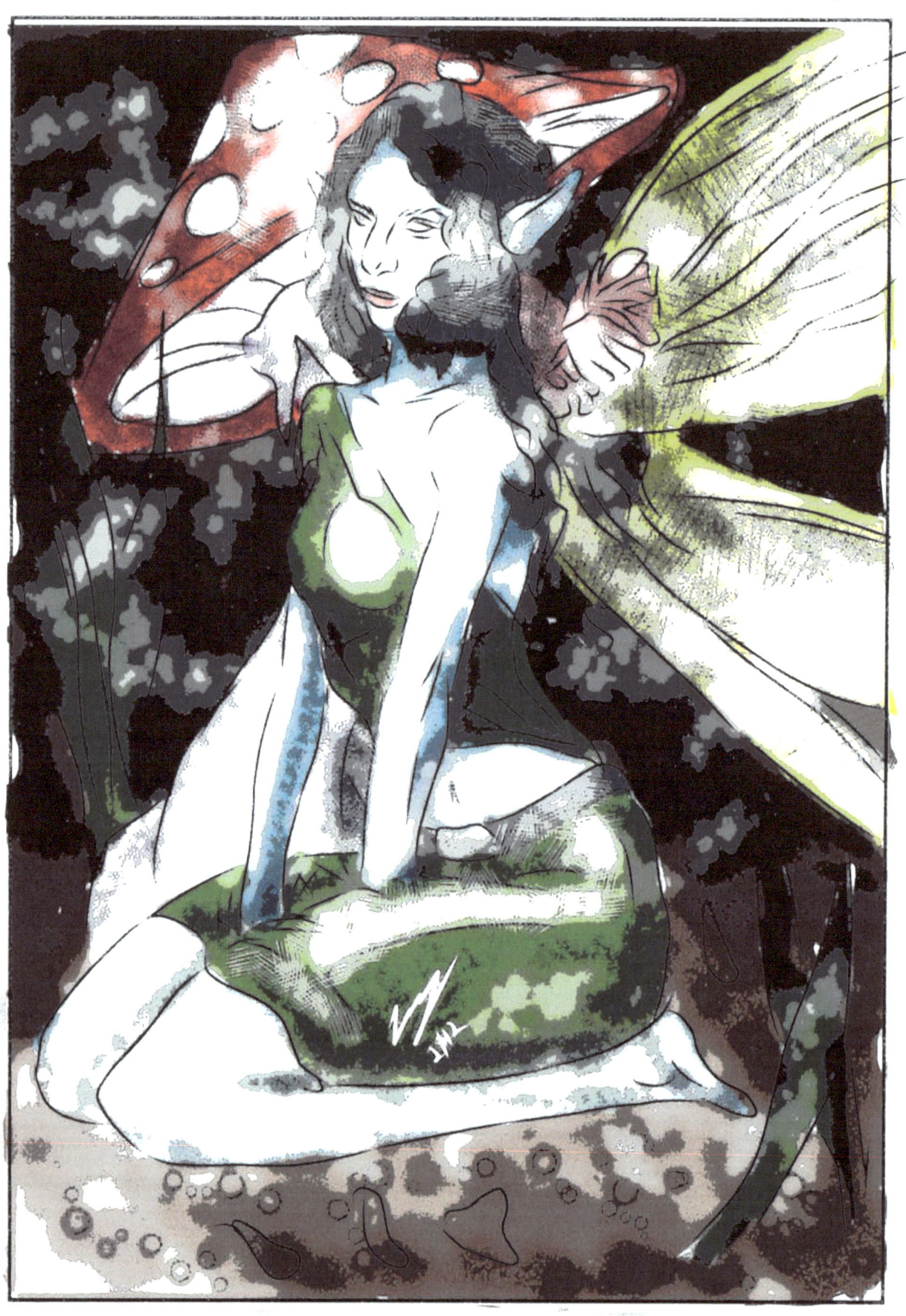

Illustrated by Benjamin Long 2012

Figure Drawings

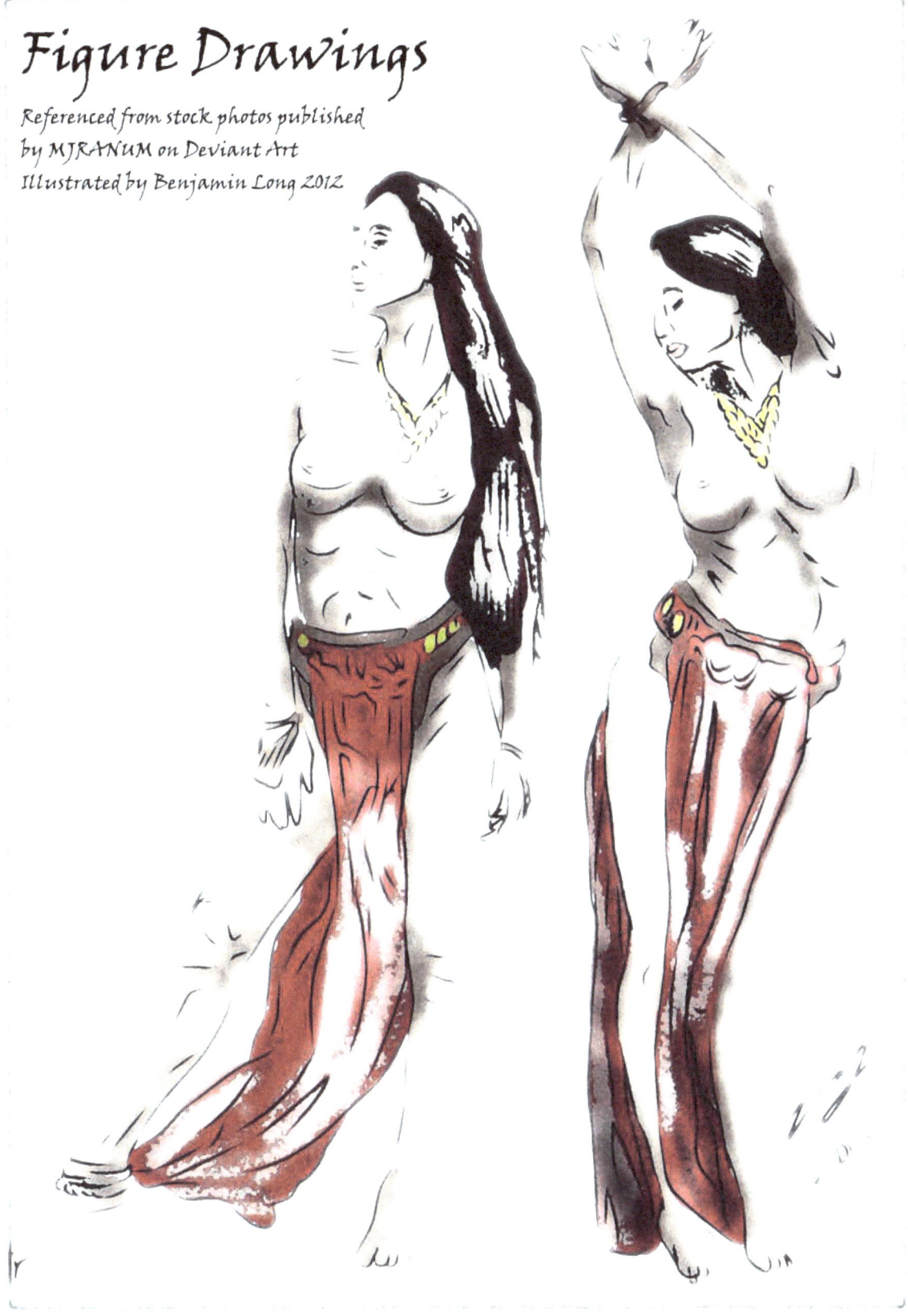

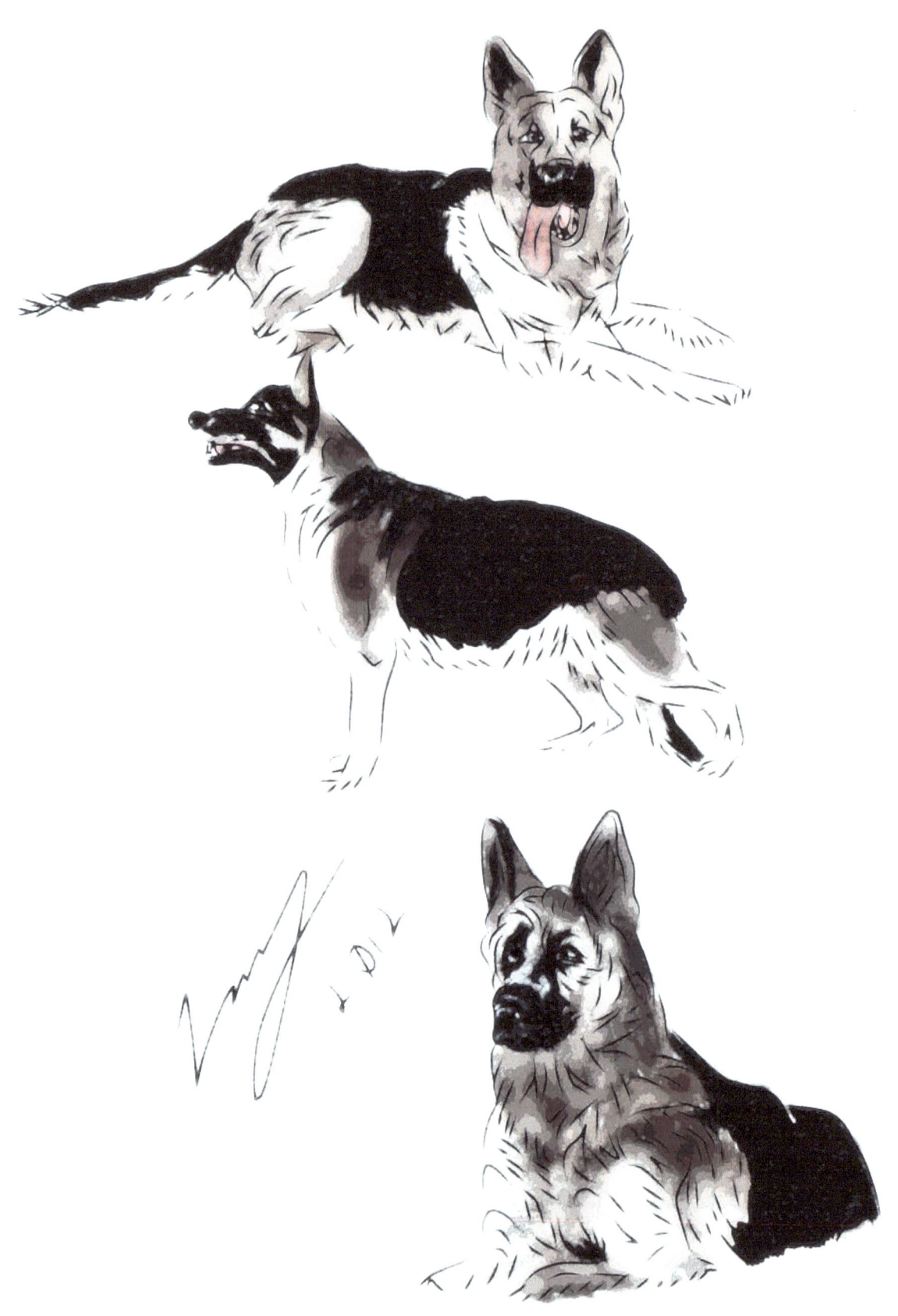

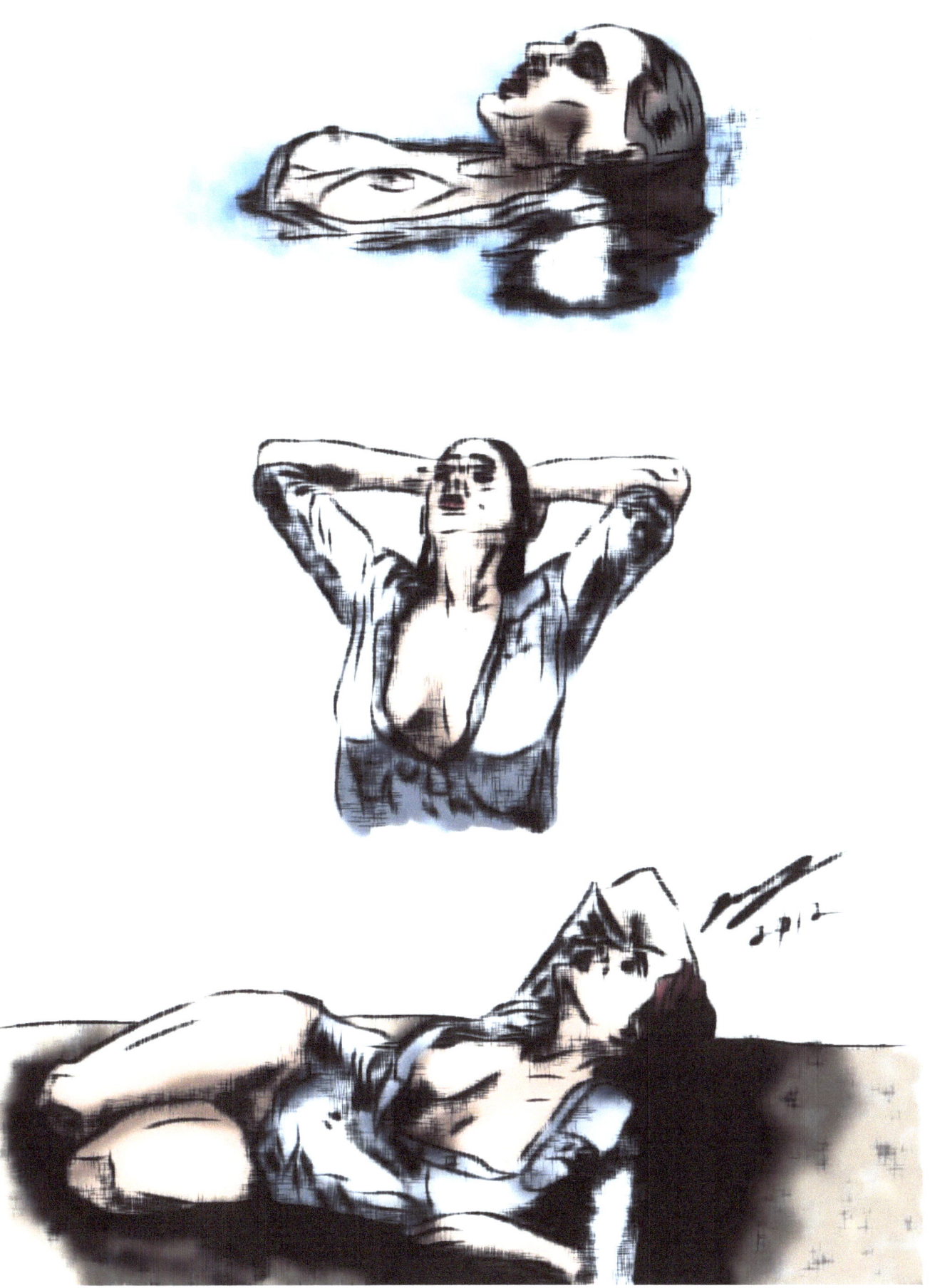

Twin Blondes

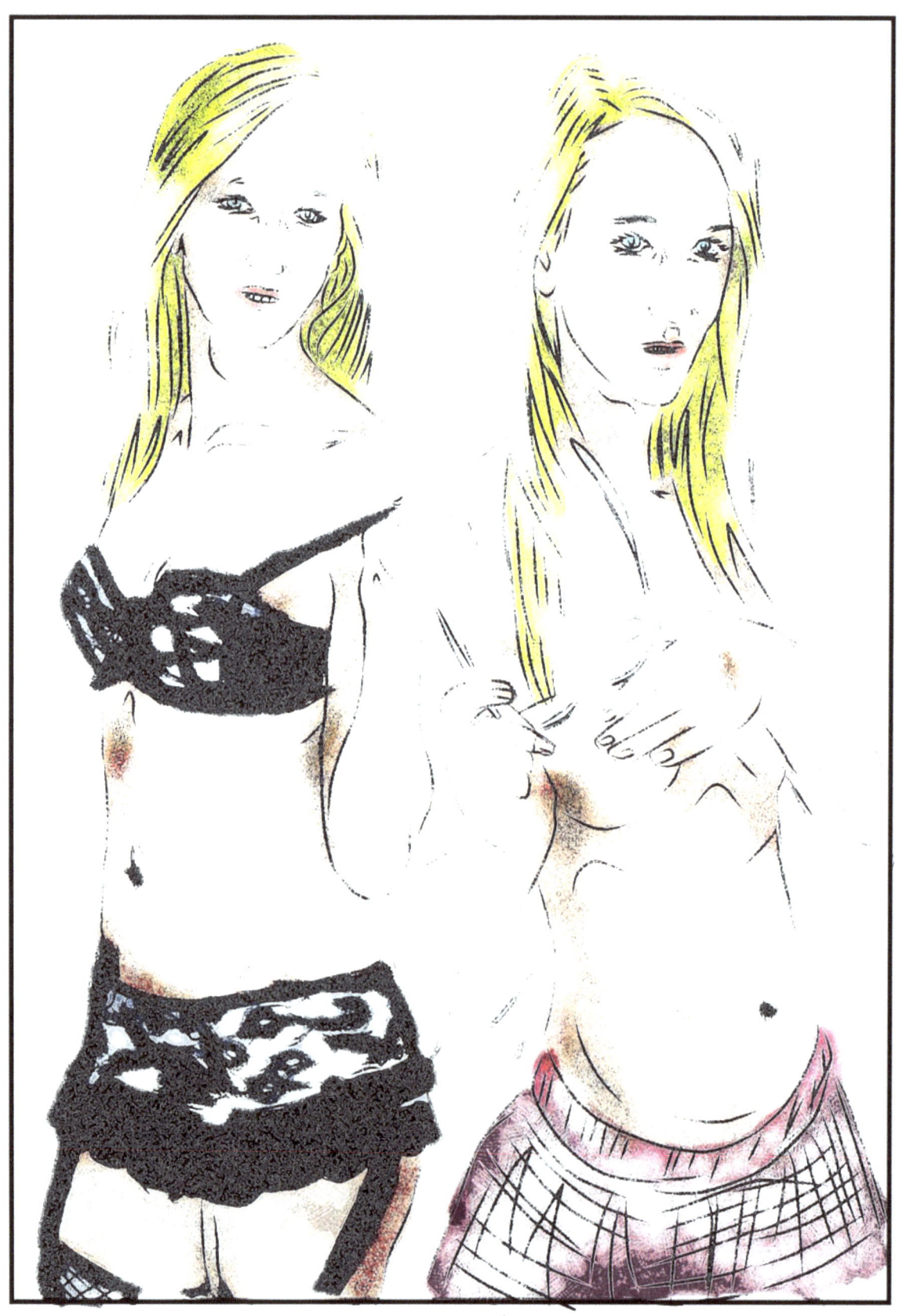

Illustrated by Benjamin Long 2012

Little Ringed Plover

Charadius dubious

Illustrated by Benjamin Long 2012

Heathen Art LLC

Benjamin Long, **Illustrator**

The pieces of artwork contained within are the property of Heathen art and Benjamin R Long. No image may be duplicated in part or whole without written permission of Benjamin Long.

Copyrighted images are protected under Title 17 of the USC and traditional copyright applies and duplications must be made in accordance with US law regarding the "Fair use " clause.

Benjamin Long may be contacted on the following Forums:

E-Mail: wiking88142001@yahoo.com

Skype: whitewolfheathen

http://whitewolfheathen.deviantart.com/

Commission rates :

Rough Sketch $8 USD

Digital Drawing/Painting $25 USD

Traditional Drawing/Painting on Canvas Panel 8x10 $35 USD

Traditional Drawing/Painting on Canvas Panel 16x20 $80 USD

www.ingramcontent.com/pod-product-compliance
Lightning Source LLC
Chambersburg PA
CBHW051105180526
45172CB00002B/783